Women Entrepreneurship in India

Women Entrepreneurship in India

Edited by

Jaynal Ud-din Ahmed
Professor, Department of Management,
North-Eastern Hill University, Tura Campus, Tura, Meghalaya

and

Khundrakpam Devananda Singh
Assistant Professor, Department of Management,
North-Eastern Hill University, Tura Campus, Tura, Meghalaya

New Century Publications
New Delhi, India

NEW CENTURY PUBLICATIONS
4800/24, Bharat Ram Road,
Ansari Road, Daryaganj,
New Delhi - 110 002 (India)

Tel.: 011-2324 7798, 4358 7398, 6539 6605
Fax: 011-4101 7798
E-mail: indiatax@vsnl.com • info@newcenturypublications.com
www.newcenturypublications.com

Editorial office:
LG–7, Aakarshan Bhawan,
4754-57/23, Ansari Road, Daryaganj,
New Delhi – 110 002

Tel.: 011-4356 0919

First Published: **July 2016**

ISBN: **978-81-7708-425-2**

Published by New Century Publications and printed at Salasar Imaging Systems, New Delhi.

Designs: Patch Creative Unit, New Delhi.

PRINTED IN INDIA

About the Book

According to Census 2011, population of India increased from 103 crore in 2001 to 121 crore in 2011, an increase of 18 crore or 17.6 percent. Out of 121 crore, 62.4 crore (51.6 percent) were males and 58.6 crore (48.4) were females.

Women play a critical role in the family which is the basic unit of a society. Family is a strong force for social cohesion and integration and as such should be strengthened. The inadequate support to women and insufficient protection to their respective families affect society as a whole and undermines efforts to achieve gender equality. In different cultural, political and social systems, various forms of family exist and the rights, capabilities and responsibilities of family members must be respected.

The extent of empowerment of women in the national hierarchy is determined largely by three factors: their economic, social and political identity. These factors are deeply intertwined and interlinked with many cross cutting linkages. However, if efforts in even one dimension remain absent or weak, outcomes generated by the other components are adversely affected. Women can be truly empowered only when all the three factors are simultaneously addressed and made compatible with each other. In other words, for holistic empowerment of women to happen, economic, social and political aspects impacting women's lives must converge effectively.

A growing body of work shows that entrepreneurial behaviour is dependent on social and economic factors. For example, countries with healthy and diversified labour markets or stronger safety nets show a more favourable ratio of opportunity-driven rather than necessity-driven women entrepreneurs.

This volume contains 14 scholarly papers which provide deep insights into various aspects of women entrepreneurship in India.

About the Editors

Dr. Jaynal Ud-din Ahmed is presently Professor, Department of Management, North-Eastern Hill University, Tura Campus, Tura, Meghalaya. After completing his Post-graduation in Accounting and Finance, he obtained Ph.D. degree in Business Administration from Assam (Central) University, Silchar. He also holds Bachelor of Law (LL.B.) and Master of Law (LL.M.) degrees. He has successfully completed three research projects—one sponsored by the University Grants Commission (UGC), New Delhi and two other by Indian Council of Social Science Research (ICSSR), New Delhi.

Dr. Ahmed has published research papers in national and international journals, besides authoring five books and editing six books. He has attended and presented research papers at various international, national and regional seminars and conferences. He is the recipient of Best Thesis Award (2004) and Best Young Faculty Award (2005) in recognition of his teaching and research work.

Dr. Khundrakpam Devananda Singh is currently Assistant Professor in the Department of Management, North- Eastern Hill University, Tura Campus, Tura, Meghalaya. He did his M. Com. and MBA from Indira Gandhi National Open University (IGNOU), New Delhi and Ph.D. from Manipur University, Imphal.

Dr. Singh has published 2 books and 15 research papers. He has participated and presented papers at various national and international conferences/seminars. He is also engaged in two major research projects funded by ICSSR, New Delhi and NABARD, Mumbai.

Contents

Contributors

Kalkame Ch. Momin	Department of Horticulture, North-Eastern Hill University, Tura Campus, Tura, Meghalaya.
C.P. Suresh	Professor, Department of Horticulture, North-Eastern Hill University, Tura Campus, Tura, Meghalaya.
Chelsea Ch. Momin	Department of Commerce, Tura Government College, Tura, Meghalaya.
Pratibha Mohan	Research Scholar, Department of RDAP, North-Eastern Hill University, Tura Campus, Tura, Meghalaya.
Ajit Dhar Dubey	Assistant Professor, Department of MBA, Oxford College of Engineering, Bangalore.
Kuntal Chakrabartty	Assistant Professor, Pathar Pratima Mahavidyalaya, West Bengal.
Saikat Majumdar	Research Scholar, Department of RDAP, North-Eastern Hill University, Tura Campus, Tura, Meghalaya.
D.C. Kalita	Associate Professor, Department of RDAP, North-Eastern Hill University, Tura Campus, Tura, Meghalaya.
Kirankumar Loitongbam	Research Scholar, Department of Commerce, Manipur University, Imphal, Manipur.
M. Sanjoy Singh	Research Scholar, Department of Commerce, Manipur University, Imphal, Manipur.
Y.S. Singh	Assistant Professor, Department of Horticulture, North-Eastern Hill University, Tura Campus, Tura, Meghalaya.

Paul Dayo Passah Research Scholar, Department of RDAP, North-Eastern Hill University, Tura Campus, Tura, Meghalaya.

B.K. Mishra Assistant Professor, Department of RDAP, North-Eastern Hill University, Tura Campus, Tura, Meghalaya.

Darshana Goswami Doctoral Research Scholar, Department of Commerce and Journalism, Gauhati University, Guwahati, Assam.

Swapnali Baruah Researcher, Tinsukia, Assam.

Arambam Jolly Devi Assistant Professor, Department of Family Resource Management, College of Home Science, Central Agricultural University, Tura, Meghalaya.

Arambam Geetanjali Marketing Manager, BASF India Ltd., Bangalore.

Bindusar Irom Accounts Manager, Babina Hospitalities Private Limited, Imphal.

Mriganka Chakraborty Research Scholar, Department of Management, North Eastern Hill University, Tura Campus, Tura, Meghalaya.

Benjamin F. Lyngdoh Assistant Professor, Department of Tourism and Hotel Management, North-Eastern Hill University, Shillong.

Preface

An entrepreneur is an individual who organizes and operates a business or businesses, taking on financial risk to do so. An entrepreneur is commonly seen as an innovator of new ideas, and business processes. Management skills and strong team-building abilities are often perceived as essential leadership attributes for successful entrepreneurs. Leadership, management ability, and team-building are considered to be the essential qualities of an entrepreneur.

A growing body of work shows that entrepreneurial behaviour is dependent on social and economic factors. For example, countries with healthy and diversified labour markets or stronger safety nets show a more favourable ratio of opportunity-driven rather than necessity-driven women entrepreneurs. Empirical studies suggest that male entrepreneurs possess strong negotiating skills and consensus-forming abilities.

According to Census 2011, population of India increased from 103 crore in 2001 to 121 crore in 2011, an increase of 18 crore or 17.6 percent. Out of 121 crore, 62.4 crore (51.6 percent) were males and 58.6 crore (48.4) were females.

Women play a critical role in the family which is the basic unit of a society. Family is a strong force for social cohesion and integration and as such should be strengthened. The inadequate support to women and insufficient protection to their respective families affect society as a whole and undermines efforts to achieve gender equality. In different cultural, political and social systems, various forms of family exist and the rights, capabilities and responsibilities of family members must be respected.

The extent of empowerment of women in the national hierarchy is determined largely by three factors: their economic, social and political identity. These factors are deeply intertwined and interlinked with many cross-cutting linkages. However, if efforts in even one dimension remain absent or weak, outcomes generated by the other components are adversely affected. Women can be truly empowered only when all the three factors are simultaneously addressed and made compatible with each other. In other words, for holistic empowerment of women to happen, economic, social and political aspects impacting women's life must converge effectively.

The emergence and rapid multiplication of self-help groups (SHGs) based on micro credit is a phenomenon that is gaining increasing importance in the development scenario.

Despite the increased access to credit, there continues to be several hurdles faced by women when they want to access credit from banks. These include huge amounts of paperwork and the fact that women are often pressurized by banks to recover loans made earlier to men in the village as an unwritten conditionality before loans are released to them.

This volume contains 14 scholarly papers which provide deep insights into various aspects of women entrepreneurship in India.

The paper, *Role of Women in Horticulture Entrepreneurship*, authored by Kalkame Ch. Momin, C.P. Suresh, and Chelsea Ch. Momin, observes that women of the North-East have been playing a proactive role in all walks of life. However, empowering women entrepreneurs of the North-East region is essential for achieving the goals of sustainable development for which efforts are required in the development of women entrepreneurs and the participation of women in the entrepreneurial activities.

The paper by Pratibha Mohan, *Women Entrepreneurship*, examines, on the basis of secondary data that entrepreneurship is one of the processes that lead to women empowerment. There has been considerable growth of women entrepreneurship in the state of Assam.

The study titled, *Migration and Rural Entrepreneurship,* by Ajit Dhar Dubey, investigates entrepreneurship of migrants and their location choice. The study finds that social capital and social networks established in one's home region are strong factors in location of choice of entrepreneurs. Entrepreneurs from rural origins tend to choose to start their businesses in rural areas in general and half of entrepreneurs migrate back to their homes in particular to avail of local comparative advantages.

Kuntal Chakrabartty's paper, *Supply Chain Management for Rural Women Entrepreneurs,* observes that the change creates greater importance on food value chains, where small producers, especially women, tend to be more active. The study shows specifically that SEWA's effort have made women producers more professional which has enabled them to become entrepreneurs and cash on market opportunities worldwide.

The paper titled, *Rural Development through Agri-preneurship,* by Saikat Majumdar and D.C. Kalita, points out that it is essential to train the jobless agriculture graduates, youths and others, in agri-business management as agri-preneurs for their betterment as well as economic stability. Agri-preneurship is important for increasing the demand for organic quality food, improvement of livestock business, better production of fruits and vegetables, willingness to enter into the agri-business sector and to reduce malnutrition.

The paper titled, *Factors Affecting Women Entrepreneurship,* authored by Kirankumar Loitongbam and M. Sanjoy Singh, has identified the factors that affect women entrepreneurship while running SHGs. The paper has categorized the factors into economic, social, cultural, legal and administrative for women entrepreneurship in Manipur.

The paper by C.P. Suresh, Kalkame Ch. Momin, Y.S. Singh and Chelsea Ch. Momin deals with *Horticulture Entrepreneurship*, and highlights that horticulture provides much needed opportunities for diversification towards high value crops which yield higher incomes in comparison to traditional crops, thereby improving the livelihood security of the farmers in hilly areas where non-farm source of income is limited. The paper concludes with an idea that North-East India, being favourable in agro-climatic diversity, has immense opportunity for growing a large variety of horticultural crops.

Paul Dayo Passah and B.K. Mishra in their paper, *Livestock in the Livelihood of the Tribals*, examine the role of livestock-based entrepreneurship due to its multi-functional outputs and contribution to the socio-cultural security. Considering its significant contribution in terms of household income, employment generation and availability of basic needs to the people, the paper suggests an urgent need to develop livestock in order to achieve a sustainable livelihood for the people of this region.

Darshana Goswami in a case study titled, *Co-operative Entrepreneurship for the Endorsement of Ethno-Economy,* assesses the entrepreneurship movement in Lakshimpur village located in Darrang district of Assam where about 500 families of farmers became united and formed Lakshimpur Anchalik Meen Mahal Samiti for the integrated pisciculture in a single pond named Lakhimpur pukhuri. The paper is a discovery of the significance of unification of society under a single organizational roof to direct the traditional occupation through proper wealth management for sustainable ethno-economic growth and development in the modern context.

The paper by Swapnali Baruah, *Women Empowerment and Self-help Groups,* has raised the question of women empowerment and security. The paper attempts to look at women empowerment through self-help groups and their security in Assam.

The paper titled, *Entrepreneurial Skill Development for Self-employment*, by Arambam Jolly Devi and Arambam Geetanjali, has observed that the entrepreneurial education and training programmes can intervene as basic literacy programmes and work as a link between entrepreneurial development and education.

Bindusar Irom in the paper, *Entrepreneurship and Promotion of Tourism,* scrutinizes that entrepreneurship can take its shape in promotion, publicity and marketing in conformity with tourist profiles and product characteristics. The mechanism needs to come up with industry-oriented policies to boost the sector by granting incentives such as tax reforms with regard to tax holiday and exemptions which will act as a leapfrog for this sector in Manipur.

The paper by Mriganka Chakraborty, *Entrepreneurial Finance,* examines the trends of bank finance and Tea Board financial schemes for the growth of tea entrepreneurs over the years. It finds that flow of credit towards tea entrepreneurs in Barak Valley has not been at par with the national level.

The paper, *Socio-economic Impact of Tourism Entrepreneurship,* by Benjamin F. Lyngdoh finds that the main contribution of tourism entrepreneurship is in the field of socio-economic development. The paper focuses on the impact of tourism entrepreneurship on entrepreneurs who are involved in micro and small enterprises. It reveals that tourism entrepreneurship positively impacts the socio-economic outcomes of the entrepreneurs.

We take this opportunity to place on record our deep appreciation for all the contributors to this volume. Their scholarly papers would surely add to the existing body of literature on the subject and ignite debate on its various dimensions.

We also place on record our gratitude to the following scholars for their help and guidance at different stages of the completion of this work: Professor Furqan Qamar, Secretary General, Association of Indian Universities (AIU), New Delhi; Professor Eugene D. Thomas, Pro-Vice-Chancellor, North-Eastern Hill University, Tura Campus, Tura, Meghalaya; Professor M.S. Jahur, University of Chittagong, Bangladesh; Professor S. Sikidar, Gauhati University, Guwahati; Dr. Kamal Uddin Ahmed, Retired Principal, Karimganj College, Karimganj, Assam; Professor G.P. Prasain, Manipur University, Imphal, Manipur; Professor S.S. Khanka, National Institute of Financial Management (NIFM), Faridabad, Haryana and Professor G. Singaiah, Department of Management, North-Eastern Hill University.

NEHU, **Jaynal Ud-din Ahmed**
Tura Campus **Khundrakpam Devananda Singh**

1

Role of Women in Horticulture Entrepreneurship

Kalkame Ch. Momin, C.P. Suresh and Chelsea Ch. Momin

Role of Women in Agriculture

Rural women form the most important productive workforce in the Indian economy. Beyond the conventional market-oriented narrower definition of *productive workers*, almost all women in rural India can be considered as *farmers* in some sense, working as agricultural labourers, unpaid workers in the family farm enterprise, or combination of the two. Moreover, several farm activities traditionally carried out by men are also being undertaken by women as men are pulled away into higher paying employment. Thus, rural India is witnessing a process which could be described as feminization of agriculture.

Despite significant contribution of women in the production process, an all pervasive bias of development planners in treating them primarily as consumers of social services rather than producers, kept them away from the development programmes in agriculture and allied sectors. As men and women have different roles and needs and face gender-specific constraints, women may not automatically benefit from development activities, but may remain excluded.

In spite of the key role of women in crop husbandry, animal husbandry, fisheries, horticulture, forestry and post-harvest technology, those in-charge of formulating packages of technologies, services and public policies for rural areas have often tended to neglect the productive role of women.

Consequently, developments in technology, specifically tailored to women-specific occupations and the involvement of women in technology development and transfer have received inadequate attention from both scientific and administrative departments of the government.

Women have traditionally been discriminated in their access to productive resources and have been denied ownership of land, cattle, trees, harvest and shelter. They have even been discriminated in access to credit and marketing facilities for their economic activities. It is, thus, essential to develop strategies and mechanism to improve women's access to agricultural support services.

It has been recognized that for an accelerated socio-economic development of any community, the active participation of women in the entire process is very essential. In a social set up like ours, the participation of women in the development process has to be ensured through tangible measures, taken at various levels, which will result in empowerment of women in the real sense. In view of the above, government has taken a conscious view to make adequate provisions in its policies and programmes through which it is ensured that the women of the country are empowered and they become active participants in the development process.

The absence of faster diversification is partly due to the lack of new economic opportunities for women. While men migrate to take up new employment opportunities in rural areas, women find themselves at a disadvantage.

There appears to be a faster rate of occupational mobility out of agriculture among men than among women. The latter remain more bound to rural areas and to agriculture due to socio-cultural and structural causes.

Importance of Land for Women

Land is important for women due to following reasons:

1. Land access can reduce a household's risk of poverty, but

for persistent gender inequalities, land solely in men's hands need not guarantee female welfare.

2. Direct land transfers to women are likely to benefit not just women but also children. Evidence, both from India and from many other parts of the world, shows that women, especially in poor households, spend most of the earnings they control, on basic household needs, while men spend a significant part of theirs on personal goods, such as alcohol, tobacco etc.
3. Women with assets such as land have greater bargaining power, which can lead to more gender-equal allocations of benefits even from male incomes.
4. Women without independent resources are highly vulnerable to poverty and destitution in case of desertion, divorce, or widowhood. In parts of western and north-western India, rural women even from rich parental and marital families, deprived of their property shares when widowed, can be found working as agricultural labourers on the farms of their well-off brothers or brothers-in-law. The fate of deserted and divorced women is worse.
5. Tenure security, and especially titles, can empower women to assert themselves better with agencies that provide inputs and extension services.
6. Women in many parts of South Asia are often better informed than men about traditional seed varieties and the attributes of trees and grasses. If they have greater control over land and farming, this knowledge can be put to better use.

Sources of Land for Women

There are three main sources of land for women:

1. Direct government transfers.
2. Market purchase/lease.
3. Inheritance or gifts from families.

To enhance women's land access from all three sources, a range of initiatives are needed, including land titles to women in all government land transfers, credit support to poor women to purchase or lease in land from the market, raising legal awareness and legal support about women's inheritance rights. It will also need a new approach to enable women to retain the land they get by strongly encouraging a *group approach* in land cultivation and investment in productive assets. It is now well-recognized that the poor are best empowered if they function as a group rather than as individuals. This lesson should be incorporated in the creation of all productive assets in women's hands.

Agricultural policies are of prime importance in gender budgeting exercises as there is a growing feminization of agriculture in recent years with out-migration of men to urban areas in search of work. The number of women-headed households in the agricultural sector is also increasing. The prosperity of agriculture therefore will largely depend on how effectively these women are empowered.

Enhancing women's rights to land, providing infrastructure support to women farmers and advancing legal support on existing laws are some of the policy interventions needed. However, critical problems persist. The lack of formal titles to women on the land they cultivate is a big drawback. This adversely affects their access to credit, inputs and marketing outlets. It also reinforces women's position as unpaid farm labourers, which reduces their incentives to invest in the land. It further excludes them from receiving agricultural extension services, new production techniques etc.

The lack of appropriate women-friendly tools and agricultural implements is another drawback. Also, the co-operatives of farmers basically comprise of men and therefore disadvantageous to women in terms of mindset and location and services profile. The agricultural policy, therefore, needs to be reviewed to provide a gender-friendly perspective.

Policies for non-farm sector and information is another highly important area that has to be seriously reviewed keeping in view the gender perspective. As women tend to remain in the rural sector they also undertake non-farm activities, which significantly contribute to the family's income. In times of agricultural stress, it is these non-farm activities of women that support the family. Therefore, the requirements of women in this sector need to be identified and appropriate support facilities in terms of access to raw materials, micro credit, skill development, training, market linkages etc. have to be ensured.

Motivational Factors for Women Entrepreneurs

Motivational factors influencing women to join the leading group of entrepreneurs are of two types. One is entrepreneurship by choice, and the other is entrepreneurship by necessity. Women become entrepreneurs by choice due to the following factors:

1. To materialize their idea into a capital.
2. For their empowerment and freedom.
3. To prove their worth among their male family members.
4. To establish their own rules for their work.
5. To overcome the deficiencies they faced during their job experience.
6. Economic independence.
7. Establishing their own creative ideas.
8. Establishing their own identity.
9. Achievement of excellence.
10. Building self-confidence.
11. Developing risk taking ability.
12. Equal status in the society.
13. Greater freedom and mobility.

Prospects of Horticulture for Women Entrepreneurship

One of the most eco-friendly sites in the map of India, North-East is perhaps the most untapped minefield of potential resources. This isolated and mysterious land of natural abundance, have a host of wonders to offer for entrepreneurs and for womenfolk, in particular. The North-Eastern region of

India is unique in terms of its indigenous population, strong cultural practices and traditional trading background, especially by women. It is also worth mentioning here that the state of Meghalaya strongly pursues the matrilineal practice which allows them to enjoy property and other rights, as well as give them the freedom to participate in any social, cultural, religious, political or economic activity and have a great potential for successful entrepreneurship—but yet to be fully exploited for economic development.

Like most women entrepreneurs in India, these women from the North-East region have also embarked on their entrepreneurial journey on a relatively smaller scale, mostly based out of their homes. They began with traditionally women-oriented business like beauty and well-being, garments, fashion, handloom and handicrafts etc., mostly without any formal training or a rigid business framework. Women from the region have realized the potential resources of the region and have initiated various entrepreneurial activities in order to tap the natural wealth of this region. Women of the North-East are now playing a proactive role in all walks of life but in the field of business, it has not been a very easy journey for them to enter the threshold of a man's arena.

Women constitute a major component of agricultural workforce. They have, however, lagged behind in use of improved crop production and processing tools and machinery. Now, a number of gender neutral and simple devices/equipment for crop production and processing has been developed. Their adoption by women will not only help improve agricultural production but will also elevate the status of women through better jobs and greater role in the economy. Agro and food processing industry is another area for entrepreneurship in the North-East region, especially mushroom cultivation, which is a flourishing area.

Moreover, entrepreneurs can venture into areas like agriculture, horticulture, fisheries, poultry, animal husbandry and forestry which would improve value addition in the agricultural produce and employment generation in the region. As entrepreneurs, women of North-East region are taking lead in establishing horti-based industries and providing job for their fellow women. Being farmers, women are becoming very active in improving their farm productivity as well as their net income.

Areas for Entrepreneurship

Some of the areas for successful enterprise in the North East region are as follows:

Cultivation of Organic Fruits and Vegetables: The farmers of the region are, by and large, engaged in organic cultivation, particularly in the upland ecosystem. With the changing attitude of the people living in metropolitan cities towards consumption of organic fruits and vegetables, womenfolk of North-East region can take advantage of this situation and create a market for organic fruits and vegetables which will also help them to get higher prices for their produce.

Setting Up of Horticulture Nursery: There has been an increasing demand for horticultural crops, more particularly fruits, both in urban and rural areas of India. With this, the demand for good quality planting materials has gone up and hence the nursery business has developed rapidly in the recent years in the country. Nursery products are no longer restricted to orchards or large parks and gardens. It has entered into high rise buildings, offices, factories, business houses, hospitals, hotels, backyards, roadsides in cities, roof tops, etc. for decoration purposes also. Ornamental nursery business, therefore, has come up on a large scale in areas near cities and towns and women in particular can opt for such kind of enterprise to enhance their livelihood.

Floriculture and Landscaping: The North-East region has a vast diversity of flora including orchid and wild native ornamentals. There is little entrepreneurial activity here but there is potential to develop it, based on the natural resources available locally. Floriculture has been proposed as an ideal basis for sustainable enterprise development for resource-poor communities—whether remote, rural or peri-urban areas. For instance, ornamental plants that grow here can be made into value added products like dried flowers, bouquets, perfumes, potpourri, rose water, etc. Taking advantage of the local flora, which will require less maintenance and is easily available, one can also take up landscaping as a business.

Mushroom Cultivation: Mushroom growing, which is an indoor activity, is one activity in which women can play a vital role without sacrificing their household responsibilities. Mushroom cultivation is simple, low cost and suitable for rural areas, is labour intensive and can provide employment for the semi-urban and rural people. Mushroom cultivation will improve the socio-economic condition of the farmers, families and solve employment problems of both literate and illiterate, especially women.

Low Cost Nutritional Foods: A large number of low cost nutritional products grouped under infant food, health beverages, nutritious snacks, convenience foods (even for people on fast), speciality foods (for patients under stress condition) and home preserves have been developed which require simple processing methods and have the ability to fulfil the nutritional requirements of our population, especially the vulnerable segments of the society. Babycorn, quality protein maize, nutritional grains, etc. are the gift for people under stress conditions and can be used to develop a number of products. These products are a great source of rural entrepreneurship, particularly suited to women, due to low capital requirements.

Coconut Sector: Coconut plantation plays an important role in the rural economy by generating income and employment. It is a major sector, which is women-dominated. The role of women in the coir sector is as high as 80 percent and 60 percent in coconut processing and broom making, respectively. Involvement of women in coconut based handicrafts is up to 40 percent. Women generally work as groups and hence, there is need to organise women's societies with a view to empower women, socially and economically.

Processing for Additional Income: Horticulture as a source of cheap raw material and being perishable, it needs processing when there is bumper production or glut in the market. Commodities like pineapple, litchi, tomato, mango, passion fruit, jackfruit, etc. have the potential for value addition by preparing jams, jellies, squash, ketchup and chips. There has to be some kind of processing to add value to the above said produce, which will lead to better income and employment of women. Many simple farm produce processing technologies have been developed using minimum equipment and small investments. Women should be trained with some skilled development programmes for handling these equipments.

Conclusion

"A woman is the full circle, within her is the power to create, nurture and transform". Therefore, empowering women entrepreneurs of the North-East region is truly essential for achieving the goals of sustainable development of the nation in totality. Right efforts from all areas are required in the development of women entrepreneurs and their greater participation in the entrepreneurial activities. Government should extend better educational facilities, suitable financial schemes, training for technical and management skills and professional competence to womenfolk. On the part of the society, incessant support and recognition is equally essential.

Though the current situation in North-East region is not extraordinarily brilliant, the paradigm shift is visible and we can definitely expect the best in the near future. Women have the potential and determination to set up, uphold and supervise their own enterprise in a very systematic manner and appropriate support and encouragement from the society, family and government can make these women entrepreneurs a part of the mainstream of national economy and they can contribute to the economic progress of India. Entrepreneurship is all about innovation and risk taking and with abundant opportunities offered by the land, North-East India can be a haven for entrepreneurs.

There is need to design programmes which could gainfully utilise the services and skills of women in relation to their involvement in horticulture based allied activities. This would also help in generating self-employment and rural entrepreneurship. Some of the ventures could be agri-service centres for sale of quality seeds and other agricultural inputs; advisory services and consultancy; village-level marketing; multipurpose warehouses and controlled atmosphere storage; hiring of implements; micro propagation; production of bio-fertilisers; bio-control agents; food processing and testing units; post-harvest management units; agri-horticulture; cultivation and management of medicinal and aromatic plants; utilisation of crop residues; mushroom cultivation etc.

Entrepreneurship skills can help in building confidence and self-awareness through income generation. Various activities can be taken up by rural women for income generation while being at home and by organising themselves in 'self-help groups'.

References

Brush, C. and Gatewood, E.J. (2008), "Women Growing Businesses: Clearing the Hurdles", *Business Horizons,* 51(3): 175-180.

Dhameja, S.K. (2002), "Women Entrepreneurs: Opportunities, Performance and Problems", Deep and Deep Publishers, New Delhi.

Goyal, M. and Parkash, Jai (2011), "Women Entrepreneurship in India: Problems and Prospects", *International Journal of Multidisciplinary Research*, 1(5): 195-207.

Khalim, A. (2012), "Women Entrepreneurship: The Emerging Workforce in 21st Century, Turning Challenges into Opportunities", Proceedings of 2nd International Conference on Business Management, 1-23.

Sharma, Y. (2013), "Women Entrepreneur in India", *IOSR Journal of Business and Management*, 15(3): 9-14.

Mustafa, Z. (2013), "Prospects and Challenges of Women Entrepreneurship: A Study of the Women Entrepreneurs of Jammu and Kashmir", *Journal of Research in Commerce and Management*, 2(6): 78-91.

2

Women Entrepreneurship

Pratibha Mohan

Acceleration in rural development is interlinked with entrepreneurship. Defining it is not an easy task, as many words correlate with the meaning of entrepreneurship including innovation, risk taking and even owning and managing small business. A person creating new combinations of production factors in newer markets and in newer organizational forms is known as an entrepreneur. He is also termed as a person who is willing to take risks by exploiting market opportunities and operating a business on his own. Entrepreneurship is most important for the rural areas as it is necessary to bear in mind that the entrepreneurial skills are required to improve the quality of life for individuals, families and communities.

Women Entrepreneurship

Entrepreneurship has always intrigued researchers over the years as it is hard to define. It has generally been assumed, however, that an entrepreneur is a male. Historically and traditionally, women have been confined to the private sphere of the household, doing the daily chores and tending to the family needs. Therefore, they have been denied access to the requisite resources for entrepreneurial entry—access to capital, business and technical education, and prior management experience. A women entrepreneur, in general terms, can be defined as any individual woman or a group of women, who initiate, organize and operate a business enterprise. Government of India has defined women entrepreneurship as an enterprise owned and controlled by a women having a minimum financial interest of 51 percent of the capital and giving at least 51 percent of employment generated in the enterprise to women.

The modern concept of women entrepreneurship took shape in this region of the country in the 1980s. Contrary to the popular notion that women from the North-East (NE) are still backward, they have come a long way now and have established themselves as successful and thriving entrepreneurs not only in the region but also beyond the boundaries of the nation. In the North-Eastern region of India, methodical efforts in entrepreneurship development began in the 1970s and Assam has been the pioneer in this field. In 1973, Assam started a novel experiment on entrepreneurship development by setting up district level agencies known as entrepreneurial motivational training centres (EMTCs) to identify, select, and train prospective entrepreneurs and provide them all support services to start and run their enterprises.

Like most women entrepreneurs in India, these women from the NE region have also embarked on their entrepreneurial journey on a relatively smaller scale, mostly based out of their homes. They began with traditionally women-oriented businesses like beauty parlour and well-being, garments, fashion, handloom and handicrafts etc., mostly without any formal training or a rigid business framework.

In Assam, industries like tea, cane and bamboo, terracotta, pottery, metal works of brass and bell, wood carvings and weaving and toys have immense prospects. The work of making *Japi* is also popular in Assam. Furniture pieces of cane and bamboo are exclusive to Assam and are exported. The skills in terracotta has resulted in manufacturing of idols of Gods and mythological creatures and the pottery tradition in Assam has resulted in wonderful items like earthen pots and pitchers, plates, incense stick holders and earthen lamps. Assam also fashions many types of toys like clay toys, pith, wooden and bamboo toys, cloth toys and cloth-and-mud toys.

Besides, cotton, 'eri', 'pat' and 'muga' silk are the weaving heritage of the region.

Women from the region have realized the potential resources of the region and have initiated various entrepreneurial activities in order to tap the natural wealth of the region.

Handloom and handicrafts have been playing an important role in the economies of the NE states. According to a study sponsored by NEDFI (2002), NE contributes 19.18 percent of the total number of handicrafts units produced in India, 21.71 percent in terms of artisans and 79.58 percent in terms of value of production. Every state in the region has some unique items of production that have been highly appreciated within the country and also abroad. Handloom and handicrafts products from the NE have excellent brand value. Thus, entrepreneurship development plays a vital role for economic growth and development of a nation or a region within the nation. Out of many important benefits of entrepreneurship development, generation of employments opportunities for job seekers is one of the most important issues. The number of job seekers has increased from year to year in most of the states of India and the government cannot afford jobs for all the job seekers in the public sector. Entrepreneurship development is one of the most important measures to reduce this problem. Keeping the above facts in mind, the present paper is an attempt to highlight women entrepreneurship in Assam.

The objectives of this paper are: (a) to study the growth of entrepreneurship among women and (b) to study the problems of the growth of entrepreneurship among women.

The present study is mainly based on the secondary data which was collected from different sources like various statistical handbooks, internet and journals etc.

Results and Discussion

Women in Traditional Work Pattern in Assam: Rural women's life in Assam has greater mobility in their work pattern and social position than in other parts of the country. The women of *Karbi, Bodo, Kacharis, Mishings* and the Assamese women are enjoying relative autonomy with regard to their income earnings. Earnings of unmarried young women are not appropriated by other family members. They normally save for investment in pigs, goats or yarn for weaving.

While income from women's economic activities is not really earned in cash, a system of barter and loan is widespread at the village level. A typical example is the practice of women weaving five *gamosas* (towels) for customers, but keeping two of them as fee. This fee is known as *adhi.*

Additionally, work in the form of traditional labour collectives by *mahila samitis*, has bought much improvement in their economic status. An interesting instance of collective work was noticed among the tribal communities of Assam who run paddy banks. Under the system, young women from several households pool their share of grain and offer it on loan. Any needy person can borrow from this stock; the borrower gets six months to repay the loan along with an interest amounting to half the quantity that the person borrows. This way the paddy bank swells quickly. Women members of the paddy bank claim their share whenever the occasion arises. Very often they sell the entire quantum of paddy and buy yarn for weaving with that money (Behal, 2009).

Women in Workforce: The women participation in the workforce has been increasing over the decades. This was mainly due to the increase in literacy rate over the years. Data reveals that female work participation rate reached 22.3 percent of the work force in 1991 increasing from 19.7 percent during 1981 (Tables 2.1, 2.2 and 2.3).

However, the women participation rate is below the male participation rate. But the female participation rate as main workers was very low compared to males. However, the participation of women as marginal workers was more than those of male workers during 1991 and 1981. The female workers were mainly confined to the rural areas. They have been playing a great role in rural areas by participating in the workforce. Although their rate of participation is less, their service as workers is very important in the development of economy as well as the society.

Table 2.1: Distribution of Main and Marginal Workers in Assam, 2001 Census

Workers	Persons	Male	Percent	Female	Percent
Total Workers	95,38,591	68,70,960	72	26,67,631	27.9
Main Workers	71,14,097	58,49,032	82.21	12,65,065	17.7
Marginal Workers	24,24,494	10,21,928	42.15	14,02,566	57.8

Table 2.2: Sex-Wise Distribution of Workers and Percentage of Cultivators, Agricultural labourers, Workers in Household Industry and Other Workers by States: 2001 Census

State/Union Territory	Male/ Female/ Total	Total Workers	Percentage to Total Workers			
			C	AL	HI	OW
All-India	Male	275,014,476	31.06	20.85	3.18	44.92
	Female	127,220,248	32.93	38.87	6.46	21.75
	Total	402,234,724	31.65	26.55	4.22	37.59
Assam	Male	6,870,960	38.34	12.12	1.95	47.60
	Female	2,667,631	41.11	16.16	7.91	34.82
	Total	9,538,591	39.11	13.25	3.62	44.03

C = Cultivator; AL = Agricultural Labourers; HI = Household Industry; OW = Other Workers

Source: Office of the Registrar General, India.

Women in the Labour Force: Women had a significant contribution in the labour force as the 66th Round Survey of NSSO (2009-10) showed that female participation rate in rural areas declined to 243 per thousand as compared to 299 in the 55th Round (1999-2000).

About 85 percent of the women workers were engaged in agricultural and allied activities in rural areas of the country. A significant portion of women were engaged in the unorganized sector industries, petty trade and services and building and construction activities in urban areas (Anonymous, 2009-10).

Table 2.3: Work Participation Rate in Assam (Percentage to Total Population)

Types Aspects	Total Workers		Main Workers		Marginal Workers	
	1991	1981	1991	1981	1991	1981
Total Workers	37.5	36.7	34.2	33.5	3.3	3.2
Males	51.6	52.6	51.0	51.6	0.6	1.0
Females	22.3	19.7	16.0	14.1	6.2	5.6
Rural	40.1	38.8	35.8	34.8	4.3	4.0
Males	52.6	53.8	51.9	52.6	0.7	1.2
Females	26.6	23.1	18.8	16.1	8.0	6.9
Urban	30.2	30.0	29.5	29.2	0.7	0.8
Males	48.9	49.1	48.6	48.5	0.4	0.5
Females	9.2	8.3	8.2	7.3	1.0	1.0

Source: Statistical Outline of India, 2001-2002, p. 36.

Contribution to the Economic Sector: The Census of 1991 and 2001 revealed that the contribution of female workers in the workforce was much less than that of male workers. The paying rates of female workers were also less as compared to male workers.

The only positive change in female employment in primary sector was the marginal growth in employment in allied agricultural activities such as livestock, fishery, forestry, and mining activities. But female workers did play a significant role in the economic sector. This is clear from Table 2.4.

The Konoklota Mahila Urban Co-operative Bank Ltd. in Jorhat, Assam has ushered in a new era of rural banking. Facilitating micro banking, advancing micro credit and providing micro insurance facilities, the all-women set up bank is going all out to make rural women become self-reliant.

Table 2.4: Economic Classification of Main Workers: 1981-1991 (Percentage to Total)

Activities	Total		Males		Females	
	1991	1981	1991	1981	1991	1981
Primary Sector						
Cultivators	38.4	41.5	39.6	43.6	34.2	33.1
Agricultural labourers	26.4	25.1	21.1	19.7	44.9	46.3
Livestock, forestry, fishing, plantations, and allied activities	1.9	2.2	2.0	2.3	1.6	1.8
Mining and quarrying	0.6	0.6	0.7	0.6	0.3	0.3
Secondary Sector						
Manufacturing, processing, servicing etc.	10.2	11.3	10.9	12.1	7.5	8.2
Household industry	2.4	3.5	2.1	3.2	3.5	4.6
Construction	1.9	1.7	2.3	1.9	0.7	0.9
Tertiary Sector						
Trade and commerce	7.5	6.3	9.0	7.4	2.2	2.0
Transport, storage and communication	2.8	2.8	3.5	3.3	0.3	0.4
Other services	10.2	8.6	10.8	9.0	8.3	6.9
Total main workers	279.9	220.7	216.0	175.9	62.9	44.8

Source: Statistical Outline of India, 2001-2002.

The Bank recently launched a customer service centre at Dhekorgorah under the North-west Jorhat Development Block. With over 2,280 beneficiaries, the bank disbursed a significant amount of over ₹ 210 million as loan. 30 percent of the loans were given to self-help groups and the other 70 percent to facilitate women entrepreneurs. Set up in 1998 by a group of rural women, the Konoklota Mahila Urban Co-operative Bank Ltd. has been operating under license obtained from Reserve Bank of India since 2000.

Vocational Training for Women: The Women's Vocational Training programme was launched in India in 1974 under the Directorate General of Employment and Training. The main aim of this programme was to increase women's employability in wage/self-employment through skill training and development. A separate women's cell was also formed for this purpose, which later developed into the Women's Occupational Training Directorate. Under this Directorate in the Central Sector, a number of institutions have been set up in different parts of the country. These institutes, which include 1 national and 10 regional vocational training institutes organize regular skill/vocational training courses at basic, advanced and post-advanced levels for women who have 10th class certificates and qualify the specified eligibility conditions laid down for various courses.

Besides the structured long-term courses, these institutes also organize need-based short-term/ad-hoc courses for general women groups—housewives, students, school drop-outs, etc. and refresher training programmes in advance skills/pedagogy for ITI instructors. Under the State sector, a network of exclusive women industrial training institutes have been set up under the administrative control of the State government which provide basic skill training courses for women. Besides the764 exclusive women industrial training Institutes (WITI's), 244 WITIs and 520 women wings in general/private sector offer training for more than 46,000 seats.

Vocational Training in Rehabilitation Centre for Women (New Concept): In the women empowerment sector, to make women job eligible, skill development training needs to be promoted. With this aim and objective, the vocational training-cum-rehabilitation centre (VTRC) concept was adopted. The details of the VTRCs along with physical target are discussed in Table 2.5.

Table 2.5: Vocational Training in Rehabilitation Centre for Women

S. No.	VTRC	Intake Capacity
1.	VTRC, Morigaon	60
2.	VTRC, Barama	60
3.	VTRC, Kachukata	30
4.	VTRC, Beltola, Guwahati	30
5.	VTRC, Boko, Kamrup	10

Women in Entrepreneurship Development

Women are now-a-days engaged in entrepreneurship activities. They have become independent by taking several enterprises as businesses of their own. The government as well as financial institutions are coming up to support women for entrepreneurship development. NABARD has implemented many programmes like REDP, ARWIND, MAHIMA, DEWTA etc. to create capacity building for skill development and enterprise management. Accordingly, women are benefited from these programmes and they play an important role by motivating other women to take up the advantages of those programmes. At present, self-help groups (SHGs) are formed everywhere mainly to create awareness among rural poor women to take up enterprise on their own for raising their standard of living and to reduce poverty. By developing women entrepreneurship, women are enjoying equality and full utilization of available human resources. Although, there is still disparity in working hours and wages of female labour. It was reported that 2/3rd of the world's work is done by women at present (Table 2.6).

Women are playing a great role in marketing sector also. Women are having greater motivating power than men in market. But the difficulties are greater for women in the marketing sector. Either the females do a lot of running about or they turn to middlemen for raw materials and finished goods (Lal Kishori, 2003). There are women entrepreneur's associations which are helping in the mobilization of women entrepreneurs and in making representations to the government. They are NAYE, FCCI, FASSI and IMC which have separate wings for women organizations. Women entrepreneurship was mainly confined to areas like food, fruits, pickles, papads, tailoring etc. in the earlier years. Now this tradition has changed. Their activities have expanded to areas like engineering, nursery education, beauty parlor, electrical, electronics and other manufacturing sectors after 1980s. Even women are coming up to take professional jobs like lawyers, doctors etc.

Table 2.6: Employment in Public and Private Sector in Assam during 2000

Sector	Men	Women	Total
A. Public Sector (Total)	4,56,185	78,912	5,35,097
Central Government	71,509	5,362	76,871
State Government	2,61,170	50,574	3,11,744
Central/Quasi-Government	66,091	11,392	77,483
State Quasi-Government	46,809	9,125	55,934
Local Bodies	10,606	2,459	13,065
B. Private Sector (Total)	3,01,572	2,74,238	5,75,810
Large Establishment (Employing 25 or more workers)	2,93,253	2,73,241	5,66,494
Small Establishment (Employing 10 to 24 workers)	8,319	997	9,316
Grand Total (A + B)	7,57,757	3,53,150	11,10,907

Source: Statistical Handbook, Directorate of Economics and Statistics, Government of Assam.

Awards to Encourage Women Entrepreneurs

With the aim of honouring the spirit of womanhood, Sreemanta Sankar Mission of Guwahati, a 28 year old voluntary organization based in Guwahati and having members from different NE states, instituted a unique felicitation program in 2013.

"Vasundhara: Celebrating Womanhood", which saw felicitation of 20 iconic women of Assam on the occasion of International Women's Day, 2013, in its second year of inception has grown into a regional level program highlighting the spirit of women power. This year, the organization instituted an award program to honour iconic women entrepreneurs from across the region including Sikkim. Titled "Vasundhara: NE Woman Entrepreneur of the Year (2012-13)" award, this pioneering effort sought to honour the women entrepreneurs of the region so that their stories of success can be emulated by others and more and more women can be encouraged to set up businesses and contribute towards economic uplift of the region.

The nominations of woman entrepreneurs in 8 states of NE India were made by authorities including banks and financial institutions, industry bodies, departments under the ministry of MSME and industry and leading media personalities working for decades in the region. A total of 84 nominations were received and out of that 50 nominations with impeccable track record were short listed by the Panel.

On 27th of February, after several hours of deliberation, the panelists made their final selection and selected the following 8 entrepreneurs:

1. Assam: Hemaprava Devi (her unit is engaged in testing and painting of LPG cylinders).
2. Arunachal Pradesh: Basamlu Krisikro (organic tea farming).
3. Nagaland: H. Lemei Phom (printing and publishing).
4. Manipur: R.K. Ongbi Poornima Devi (handloom and embroidery).
5. Mizoram: Lalmuankimi (wellness and beauty).
6. Tripura: Santa Debnath (handicrafts).
7. Meghalaya: Marina Marak (education).
8. Sikkim: Yangchen Doma Lepcha (skill development).

All the above named women entrepreneurs were invited to the award program on March 11, 2014 at the Pragjyoti-ITA

Centre for Performing Arts, Machkhowa, Guwahati.

Promoting Entrepreneurship through Trade Festivals

Promoting entrepreneurship in different ways is also one of the important tasks of different organizations that have come up with their helpful hands to promote entrepreneurship in Assam.

The Indian Institute of Entrepreneurship organized a trade festival on December 27, 2013 which continued till January 5, 2014, to promote entrepreneurship and provide impetus to small businesses in the region.

The festival aimed to provide sustainable livelihood to the micro and small businesses, targeting the households and rural sectors of the region with a hope that the initiative would provide a platform to the various businesses to understand the market needs and have direct interactions with buyers besides selling their products. A total of 40 participants from different regions participated in the fair.

Products displayed at the fair included textiles, food products, home furnishing, fashion accessories and traditional Assamese jewellery etc.

The Dirang Food Processing Centre from Arunachal Pradesh and Ri-Bhoi Strawberry Cluster for the first time produced wine from kiwi and strawberry fruits after they got training from the IIE in their villages.

Earlier, they were confined to selling fruits, but now eatables including jams, pickles were also being produced from these fruits.

Similarly, there is The North East Trade Promotion and Development Council (NETPDC) which is a dedicated and bonafide registered public charitable trust working for the economic upliftment of the region.

The annual international exposition, 5th Asom International Trade Fair was organized by the North East Trade Promotion and Development Council (NETPDC) at Maniram Dewan Trade Centre, Betkuchi, Guwahati from

December 3, 2010 to December 9, 2010. More than 428 participants took part with their innovative products ranging from handicrafts, cane and bamboo, artistic textile, wood craft, terracotta, coir, jute, khadi and other mesmerizing hand made products.

Likewise, the Disang Festival is one of the major festivals of Sivasagar District. Generally, the Disang Festival is celebrated in the first week of January where various traditional fun games are organized on the sand bed of river Disang.

Besides this, many self-made local products are exhibited including textiles, food products, home furnishings, traditional dresses, handloom products, canes and bamboo and are sold during the grand festival by certain self-help groups.

The eleventh edition of the Assam Mahotsav, a two week long annual fair, was organized in Jorhat, and provided a window to the culture of the state. More than 100 stalls were set up at the fair by participants from different parts of the country.

The stalls displayed a variety of indigenous products like handloom products, canes and bamboo and jewellery. The main objective of the festival was to promote and preserve the rich heritage of Assam. It also provided a platform to local artisans to promote their skills and talent. The fair was organized under the aegis of INTANDEM.

The ultimate goal of these festivals is to provide a platform to rural artisans to exhibit their innovative ideas to the world.

Assam Entrepreneurs Take E-commerce Route

A growing number of entrepreneurs in Assam are treading the e-commerce route to not only rake in the moolah but also promote art, craft and literature of the North-East. The trend has become apparent in the past couple of years, with online portals becoming an important medium for people to buy and sell items such as traditional paintings, jewellery, home décor, fabrics including T-shirts with fancy prints and even regional language books.

Jorhat-based Parikshit Borkotoky used to sell eco-friendly handmade items and accessories such as lampshades and handbags through eBay, till he launched his own website *www.kraftinn.com* in January last year. Their manufacturing unit is at Kenduguri where 10 artisans make home décor items from bamboo such as lampshades, candle stands and handbags. Currently, the portal's product line comprises over 100 items priced between ₹ 450 and ₹ 35,000. A majority of the customers are from the metros and big cities.

Traditional and contemporary art too, has a found a platform on *www.artexdirect.com*, which was launched by the Morigaon-based Apcom Educational and Cultural Development Society.

Mifathul Rahman, who launched *www.ordermytreat.com*, an online cake and gift delivery portal, in February 2013, says, "We have over 4,000 followers on Facebook. The response to our portal is good at present. While we have tied up with bakeries in Guwahati and a few cities across the country, we plan to market our products aggressively in central and Upper Assam as well".

The North-East also got its first regional language e-book store, *www.assamkart.com*, in September, currently selling 125 books of local publishers.

Kaushal Dugar's specialty e-commerce start up supplies freshly packaged premium teas across some of the most discerning and lucrative markets for high-end teas—Russia, US, Canada and Australia—and is now targeting Japan and China. Although he founded Teaxpress Pvt. Ltd. in 2012 with his savings of ₹ 25 lakh, he has just raised US$ 1 million in seed funding from venture capital firm Accel Partners India and Singapore-based Horizon Ventures, and plans to use that money to build a strong, back-end infrastructure for what he calls an "end-to-end supply chain".

Problems Faced by Women Entrepreneurs

Apart from the tacit assumption that women are frail and indecisive, women entrepreneurs encounter many problems in their efforts to develop the enterprises they have established. The main problems faced by the women entrepreneurs may be analyzed as below.

Shortage of Finance: Women and small entrepreneurs always suffer from inadequate financial resources and working capital. They lack access to external funds due to absence of tangible security and credit in the market. Women do not generally have property in their names.

Inefficient Arrangements for Marketing and Sale: For marketing their products, women entrepreneurs are often at the mercy of the middlemen who pocket large chunks of profit.

Shortage of Raw Materials: Women entrepreneurs find it difficult to procure raw materials and other necessary inputs. The failure of many women co-operatives in 1971 such as those engaged in basket making was mainly due to the inadequate availability of forest raw material. The prices of many raw materials are still quite high.

Stiff Competition: Many of the women enterprises have imperfect organizational setup. They have to face severe competition from organized industries and male entrepreneurs.

High Cost of Production: Another problem which undermines the efficiency and restricts the development of women enterprises is the high cost of production.

Low Mobility: One of the biggest handicaps for women entrepreneurs is mobility or travelling from place to place. Women on their own find it difficult to get accommodation in smaller towns.

Family Responsibilities: In India, it is mainly a woman's duty to look after the children and other members of the family. Their involvement in family leaves little energy and time for business. Married women entrepreneurs have to make a fine balance between business and home.

Social Attitudes: The biggest problem of a woman entrepreneur is the social attitude and the constraints in which she has to live and work. Despite constitutional equality, there is discrimination against women. In a tradition-bound society, women suffer from male reservations about a woman's role and capacity. In rural areas, women face resistance not only from males but also from elderly females who have accepted inequality.

Low Ability to Bear Risk: Women have comparatively a low ability to bear economic and other risks because they have led a protected life.

Lack of Education: In India, literacy among women is very low. Due to lack of education, a majority of women are unaware of the technological developments, marketing knowledge, etc. Lack of information and experience creates further problems in the setting up and running of business enterprises.

The above discussed problems have always stood as obstacles in the progress of women confidence level in entrepreneurship. But to overcome this is the main success.

Suggestion

The growth of women entrepreneurs requires acceleration because entrepreneurial development is impossible without the participation of women. A congenial environment is needed to enable a woman to participate actively in entrepreneurial activities. Some of these steps are discussed below:

1. Promoting gender equality to overcome discrimination of role play in family and community in rural areas.
2. Women empowerment to devise and diversify vocational training, building confidence and encouraging their changing needs and skills.
3. Education to the rural women about new marketing and business tactics.
4. Infrastructural development by the government to increase the possibility for business service provider and industrial sector to enhance the entrepreneurship of women.
5. Micro finance assistance by government to rural women on a larger scale.
6. Training on gender sensitive issues.
7. Marketing assistance by marketing the products produced

by women entrepreneurs in rural areas.

8. Conduction of trade fairs specifically to advertise the work of rural women entrepreneurs.

Conclusion

The growth of women business owners and their needs cannot be overlooked. Women entrepreneurs have increasingly played an important role in spurring job creation and economic development. Through it they not only focus their hidden talent to the world but also earn money and support their family, economically. It is a holistic approach.

The State Government tried to encourage entrepreneurship among women through different skill development schemes. Through these schemes the state government help the women financially and also provide skill-based training, which ultimately help women to become self-employed. But still they have to face challenges in upgrading their entrepreneurial activities.

However, in spite of having so many obstacles, there are some successful women who have overcome these hurdles and have become famous in the society. Developing entrepreneurship among women will be the right approach for the empowerment of women.

References

"AITF, 5th Asom International Trade Fair", available at: http://asominternationaltradefair.com/about%20us.html.

"Assam Entrepreneurs Take E-commerce Route", *The Telegraph*, Wednesday, August 28, 2013, available at: http://www.telegraphindia.com/1130828/jsp/northeast/story_17281940.jsp#.U7UKYZSSwhc.

CAPART, available at: http://capart.nic.in/lists/guwahati/july/list1.htm.

Chakravarty, Ekta (2013), "The Rural Women Entrepreneurial Edge", *IOSR Journal of Humanities and Social Science,* Volume 10, Issue 1, March-April, pp. 33-36.

Das, Marami (2012), "Women Empowerment through Entrepreneurship: A Case Study of Guwahati Municipal

Corporation", *International Journal of Computer Applications in Engineering Sciences,* Volume II, Issue I, March.

Disang Mukh Sivasagar Assam, available at: http://www.dhrubazaan.in/travel/november-26th-2013.

"Economic Survey of Assam, 2012-13", Directorate of Economics and Statistics, Assam, Planning and Development Department, Government of Assam.

"Fest to Promote Trade", *The Telegraph*, Sunday, November 18, 2012, available at: http://www.telegraphindia.com/1121118/jsp/northeast/story_16206538.jsp#.U7TyypSSwhc.

"Jorhat Holds 11th Assam Mahotsav to Promote Culture and Traditions", ANI News, December 23, available at: http://www.aninews.in/newsdetail2/story146937/jorhat-holds-11th-assam-mahotsav-to-promote-culture-and-traditions.html.

Lal, Kishori (2003), "Gender Afflictions in Entrepreneurship: Indian Context", *Women and Economic Development,* p. 259.

Monisha, Behal (2009), "Women's Lives and Work Pattern in Assam" (unpublished mimeograph, 1988). In addition, a part of the paper has been adapted from another article entitled, "Women's Organizations in Assam: An Overview of Traditional and Formal Group Dynamics", published in the *Wasteland News,* November 1992-January 1993, New Delhi.

Rao, Behara Sreenivasa (2012), "Women Entrepreneurship", Laxmi Publications.

"Skill Development and Vocational Training", Government of India, Planning Commission, New Delhi, available at: http://planningcommission.nic.in/aboutus/committee/wrkgrp11/wg11_rpskill.pdf.

"Statistical Profile of Women Labour", Labour Bureau, Ministry of Labour and Employment, Government of India, 2009-2011.

"Statistical Handbook of Assam, 1991", various issues, Directorate of Economics and Statistics, Government of Assam, Guwahati.

"Teaxpress: Assamese Entrepreneur Kaushal Dugar Using E-commerce to Supply Quality Packaged Tea", *The Economic Times*, April 20, 2014, available at: http://articles.economictimes.indiatimes.com/2014-04-20/news/49266195_1_tea-varieties-tea-business-tea-estate.

Thiruvenkatachari, K. and Lasksmi, S. (2003), "Changing Role of Gender in Economic Theory", *Women and Economic*

Development, pp. 28-38.

Vocational Training for Rehabilitation Centre for Women, Directorate of social Welfare, Assam, available at: http://socialwelfareassam.com/VocTrainings.asp.

3

Migration and Rural Entrepreneurship

Ajit Dhar Dubey

Introduction

Rural areas have been experiencing out-migration of young, educated adults, or "brain drain", for a long time. Lack of appropriate job opportunities is a major barrier for rural born, well educated migrants seeking to return home or relocate to a rural place. One way to overcome the lack of job opportunities is to create their own businesses. Increasingly, rural entrepreneurship and small business ventures have been seen as a strategy for rural development (Hoy, 1996). Rural entrepreneurship is defined by Wortman (1990) as "the creation of a new organization that introduces a new product, serves or creates a new market, or utilizes a new technology in a rural environment". While traditional strategies of recruiting and relocating businesses to rural areas are not enough to boost rural economic growth, starting and growing new businesses in rural areas can stimulate local economies by creating local jobs, providing an expanded variety of products and services, and increasing quality of life in rural areas.

However, there are obstacles to rural entrepreneurship. Low population density and remoteness results in limited local demand and makes it difficult to access educated labour, sufficient capital and infrastructure (Reynolds et al., 1995). It has been found that firm entry rate is generally lower in rural areas than urban areas (Plummer and Headd, et al., 2008). What motivates an entrepreneur to relocate to a rural area? At the present, most studies in rural entrepreneurship rely on macro data from the US Census Bureau or similar data bases

(Wortmen, 1990, Henderson, 2002) or case study methods (for example, Gladwin et al., 1989 for North Florida).

Therefore, little is known about the personal characteristics of rural entrepreneurs, how they differ from those of urban entrepreneurs, or why they choose to locate their businesses in rural areas (Wortman, 1990; Henderson, 2007).

Certainly, the type and nature of the businesses is an important factor to be considered. Not all industries arise in all locations and entrepreneurs are not equally likely to enter in all industries.

Some industries are conducive in rural areas while others are more productive in populated areas. The personal traits of an entrepreneur will also influence business location decisions.

While on an average, the level of human capital increases the likelihood of starting a business, it reduces the probability of residing in a rural location (Ucbasar et al., 2008; Arenius and De Clercq, 2005; Mills and Hazarika, 2002; Huang et al., 2002). Yet, the connect of human capital and knowledge of the resources that can be exploited in local areas is important.

Michelacci and Silva (2007) found that compared to workers, entrepreneurs tend to be local. Family background and social factors affect entrepreneurs' location decision-making. The experience of growing up in a particular community with a certain entrepreneurial climate or culture can impact both an individual's decision to become an entrepreneur and their decision about business location.

Rural residency experience may shape attitudes toward rural entrepreneurship and provide rural entrepreneurial role models. This suggests a possible link between rural entrepreneurship and return migrant entrepreneurship which has till date been overlooked in the rural development research area. Our survey can fill in the blanks by investigating rural entrepreneurs' personal traits and their location decisions and return migration decisions.

Research Objectives and Hypotheses

The research inter alia aims at the following:

1. To find out necessary skills to be inculcated amongst migrants to make them rural entrepreneurs.
2. To portray the role of stakeholders like companies, government, colleges, etc. in the development of rural entrepreneurial intent amongst migration students and especially in inculcation of entrepreneurial culture.
3. To study the structure and growth of entrepreneurship in the state.
4. To test the conceptual model proposed in the research.

To meet the objectives of the study, the following hypotheses are postulated for empirical verification in the study:

H_1: The area suffers from excessive and acute migration and under employment problem.

H_2: Persons suffering from migration are interested in taking up complementary jobs to uplift their level of living.

H_3: There is lack of innovation and entrepreneurship in the state.

Research Methodology

The primary data has been collected mainly from extensive field survey of the sample units. To obtain primary information, personal interview was conducted through well designed questionnaires especially prepared in view of the objectives of the study. The information collected from primary and secondary sources was edited, categorized and arranged in logical order. In the process, certain errors and omissions were detected and corrected subsequently. Tabular analysis was done both manually and also with the IBM 'Statistical Package for Social Scientists' (IBMSPSS).

Literature Review

Breen et al. (2012) observed financial and family issues by taking a sample of 211 female entrepreneurs from Australia.

The paper pointed out that female business owners faced the problem of getting finance, and started business with low initial capital. On the family front, self-employed women faced the problem of supervision and care for their sick children.

Bliss and Garratt (2001) examined the working of organizations for women in Poland. The paper studied various activities performed by these organizations to promote women entrepreneurs. Information was collected from 12 support organizations for women and the data collected from these organizations highlighted that the basic purpose of these organizations were to provide inputs to self-employed women in the field of professional ethics, to ensure protection of their rights and companies, to allow exchange of experiences, and other activities.

Caputo and Dolinsky (2011) studied the role of financial and human capital of household members to pursue self-employment among females. The analysis revealed that business knowledge and cooperation of spouses in family matters contribute a lot in pursuing businesses. The findings further suggested that the government should provide necessary skills to women to ensure rapid growth of entrepreneurship.

Kuratka and Richard (2001) opined that micro finance is an important agenda for empowering poor women. Micro enterprises are an integral part of planned strategy for securing balanced development of the economy and of the poor women. Rural women's participation in agro-based activities is much more than what statistics reveal. This is mainly due to the fact that most of the work done by the women at farms and home is disguised as daily chores.

Mambula (2002) analyzed the major constraints faced by SMEs (small and medium enterprises) in Nigeria. A sample of 32 small business entrepreneurs was taken. The analysis of data revealed that a majority of the SMEs faced the problem of finance and infrastructure while managing their businesses. The author recommended that small business entrepreneurs should collaborate with each other to sort out various problems faced by them. There is a need to form alliance with the government, research institutions and financial institutions, to provide appropriate training for prospective small businesses.

Punitha et al. (1999) examined the problems and constraints faced by self-employed women in the Pondicherry region. A sample of 120 women, were personally interviewed during the period from June to July 1999, of which 42 belonged to rural and 78 to urban areas. The major problems faced by the rural self-employed women were competition from better quality products and marketing problems. The problems for urban entrepreneurs were, apart from the competition from better quality products, the difficulty in getting loans. The least problems faced by both rural and urban self-employed women were ignorance about schemes, distance from markets and ignorance about agencies and institutions.

Tagoe et al. (2005) examined the financial challenges faced by the urban SMEs under the financial sector liberalization in Ghana. The main challenge faced by the urban SMEs was access to affordable credit over a reasonable period. To manage this challenge, the SMEs should manage record-keeping in an effective manner. Moreover, availability of collateral improves SMEs' access to formal credit. However, better availability of investment avenues reduces the accessibility of credit to the SMEs.

Taylor and Brooks (2010) examined the marketing practices among small New Zealand organizations by taking a sample of 427 small business owners. The findings revealed that these small firms look at the marketing practices differently from their larger counterparts. Although entrepreneurship is becoming an academic discipline and a field of study, there remains, to this day, considerable disagreement with regard what constitutes a model entrepreneurship curriculum and what courses should be taught in entrepreneurship programs. The issue of the way of teaching entrepreneurship is yet to be solved. Generally, a variety of emerging models for an entrepreneurship program can be given. Each model reflects a conceptual view of entrepreneurship education.

Over time, the gap between education and the world of work has increasingly widened. Concepts learnt in the classroom have minimal real world significance. For many students, the classroom is not connected to the world of work outside of the school. Education and knowledge cannot be delivered solely from textbooks and lectures; it must include practical, hands-on experience that challenges the students, especially in entrepreneurial studies (Ani Asmah Tajul Ariffin, 2009).

Entrepreneurship education should mainly be practically oriented and not be overloaded with theoretical expositions (Dirk De Clercq, Hans Crijns and Hubert Ooghe, 2001). The aspects in starting up and managing business cannot be taught through conventional methods such as readings, lectures or watching films (Aishah Buang and Yap Poh Moi, 2002). They added that knowledge of awareness, motivational and certain competencies can only be absorbed when students have undergone or experienced and got involved in the process of inventing new business through "negotiation" and "working with entrepreneurs".

Both methods are among the best in promoting entrepreneurship attributes to students followed by simulation method, case study, role model, working papers, thesis and writing business plans.

A qualitative approach was used by Norasmah Othman, Ahmad Azmi M. Ariffin, Mohd Fauzi Mohd. Jani and Ariffin Hj Zainal, 2008 in the study titled, "Entrepreneurial Studies in Institute of Higher Learning Methods for Delivering Entrepreneurship Education" which adopted the Rubric Assessment of National Standard Practices for Entrepreneurship Education constructed by Entrepreneurship Education Consortium in Ohio, US. To assess the method of delivering entrepreneurship education, the study used seven concepts of the Rubric Assessment as indicators. The seven concepts included:

1. Facilitating and coaching.
2. Experiential learning.
3. Problem-based learning.
4. Students as leaders.
5. People in the Community.
6. Variety of methods.
7. Lifelong learning model for entrepreneurship education.

The study found that, the methods that are highly recommended in teaching entrepreneurship education are the problem-based learning (PBL) and the experiential learning methods. Fauziah Sh. Ahmad, Rohaizat Baharun and Siti Haslinah Abd Rahman mentioned in their study that entrepreneurship education needs a different teaching instructive, hence, there are studies trying to relate it to work related learning, experiential learning, action-learning, and entrepreneurial training. In other words, entrepreneurship education is more than business management, it is about learning, which means learning to integrate experience, skills and knowledge, to get prepared to start with a new venture.

In a study on entrepreneurship behaviour amongst Malaysian University students by Norasmah Othman and Faridah, K., several suggestions on how entrepreneurship education can be useful in opening up the minds and interests of potential entrepreneurs were brought. They stressed on the reality and hands-on approach in the business world because students need to be exposed early to this real situation for better understanding and to build up their self-confidence in business. Smart partnership between institutions and the business sector were also suggested whereby students can also spend some time in firms as part of their training or practicum programme so as to introduce themselves into the business culture.

Ani Asmah Tajul Ariffin made a distinction between methods applied inside and outside the classroom. Inside the classroom, there are some classical tools which are used to teach entrepreneurship such as lectures, readings, class discussion, guest speakers, individual coaching, role plays, team teaching and teamwork. However, methods that are used to teach entrepreneurship outside the classroom aim at a close contact between students and real entrepreneurs (Faudziah Zainal Abidin AND Habshah Bakar, 2005). For example, the tools are cooperation with an incubator for new ventures, dinner with entrepreneurs, internships and interviews with entrepreneurs.

Consulting-based learning basically involves consultancy-like assistance provided by the students and experts for local SMEs which would benefit the students and also the SMEs. Business consultancy requires specific skills and an appropriate level of knowledge if consultants are to help clients identify and solve their management problems. Business consultancy is essentially about acquiring and sharing knowledge. Various methods are used to evaluate a business consultancy. Measurement can be in monetary terms and/or non-monetary terms.

University of Limerick in Ireland offers a business consulting course which offer individuals, small businesses and community groups, a consultancy service to identify and solve their business problems. Student teams act as consultants to these groups. This course provides an important mechanism for introducing students to the everyday management problems and opportunities of small businesses, particularly those at the start-up and early growth stages. On completion of this course, students have an improved understanding of the role and skills required for the consulting process and are capable of advising SMEs in a professional manner. The merits of such interactions have been demonstrated through a description of various initiatives that benefit a number of stakeholders, namely students, academics, the broader educational institutions and small firms. These merits can be achieved through the provision of entrepreneurship education.

Hynes, B. and Richardson discussed about students as

consultants who offer free consultancy to local businesses that involves faculty and students working on real problems. The client gets solutions or at least the chance to see the problems through fresh eyes, while students get genuine contacts with businesses and the chance to work on a real-world issue where a good solution can have tangible pay-offs.

Aims of Migration and Rural Entrepreneurship

According to reports produced by the Global Entrepreneurship Monitor (GEM), a high correlation exists between educational attainment, including having exposure to entrepreneurship learning, and an individual's confidence to become involved in entrepreneurial ventures (GEM, 2001; GEM, 2003). Consequently, education in general and the infrastructure to support and give access to education plays an important role in entrepreneurship development worldwide. The aim, therefore, of entrepreneurship education and learning is two-fold: to ensure that we encourage our university graduates to learn about entrepreneurship and encourage them to become involved in enterprise. The subsequent paragraphs explore how this can be achieved and we commence first with a closer examination of the three main characteristics identified by the literature for developing entrepreneurship in individuals.

According to Garavan and Barra (1994), innovators and entrepreneurs possess three major characteristics, which include: knowledge, skills and attitudes. Knowledge includes, for example, knowledge of the industry, product, technique or process (Marvel and Lumpkin, 2007). Networking skills, project management skills, financial and people skills, communications skills, decision-making skills, personal entrepreneurial skills (such as persistence and being change oriented) are just some of the skills identified by Hisrich and Peters (1998) as important to entrepreneurs. Moreover, preliminary evidence supports that attitudes, especially attitude to risk-taking, as well as psycho-social forces of the individual and the cultural context, influence entrepreneurial behaviour (Ferreira and Raposo, 2008). As a consequence, entrepreneurship learning should focus on:

- Delivering useful knowledge of entrepreneurship.
- Acquiring tools for analyzing and scanning the business environment and developing a business plan.
- Developing entrepreneurial skills, drive and talents.
- Enthusing individuals to pursue and support entrepreneurship.
- Stimulating creative thinking.
- Developing attitudes in individuals that are positively disposed to and able to cope with change.
- Encouraging and supporting new start-ups and entrepreneurial ventures (Garavan and Barra, 1994; Ferreira and Raposo, 2008).

The above illustrates the multi-faceted discipline of entrepreneurship education, its commitment to promoting creative and cross-functional thinking and the integrative and holistic approach required for delivering the aims of entrepreneurship learning (Tan and Nag, 2006). Moreover, entrepreneurship learning is aimed at individuals from across disciplines: scientists, technology specialists, professionals in the creative industries and managers in large and small organizations.

Role of HR in Rural Entrepreneurship

It is identified that the two primary roles of a learning specialist include: administrator role and the consultant role. American Society for Training and Development (1983) identified fifteen key roles for the HRD practitioner. Critical outputs for each of these fifteen roles were identified. The UK perspective in the 1970s and 1980s was developed under the Manpower Service Commission, a government body. The roles identified were mainly the trainer roles (for details, see Walton, 1999). According to Ulrich (1997), in the past few years, roles for HRM professionals were often viewed in terms of the transitional form such as operational to strategic;

qualitative to quantitative; policing to partnering; short-term to long-term; administrative to consultative; functionally oriented to business oriented, etc.

In order to create value and deliver results, HRM professionals must begin not by focusing on the activities or work of HRM but by defining the deliverables of that work. Deliverables guarantee outcomes of HRM work. In terms of deliverables, there are four key roles that HRM professionals must fulfil to make their business partnership a reality. These are the roles of strategic partner, administrative expert, change agent and employee champion. The summation of these four, results in the business partner role of HRM. In India, Venkataratnam (1992) enumerated the current and suggested role of personnel. Later, Lynton and Pareek (2000) suggested the business partner role of HR. Pareek (1997) had earlier presented the partnership role of HR with different stakeholders. Combining the above perspectives, a matrix was developed which exemplifies the overlap in research on the nature of these roles.

The review highlights the strains in the literature on strategic HR roles, which essentially say the same thing, and which are grouped into the four-role typology, with the exception of two researchers, Ulrich, and Schuler and Jackson, who refer to the business partner role and innovator and strategic role respectively. Yet, the strategic perspective on the HRM function leaves an array of questions unanswered relative to the corporate HR roles (Novicevic and Harvey, 2001) and to find answers globally there has been a great deal of research on strategic HR roles, for example, research from New Zealand (Cleland et al., 2000), Australia (Teo, 2003), Europe (Storey, 1992), Thailand (Chiraprapha and McLean, 2001) and the USA (Ulrich, 1997, 2003). The results of the HRPS-sponsored Centre for Effective Organizations study of HR in large corporations in the US argue strongly for HR taking on more of a strategic partner role (Lawler and Mohrman, 2000b, 2003).

Despite credible evidence in many countries, as is reported above, supporting the view that HR management is the key strategic issue in most organizations, HR has not been a strategic partner (Brock Bank, 1999; Lawler et al., 1995; Mohrman and Lawler, 1996). The HR function has been an administrative function headed by individuals with roles aimed at cost control and administrative activities (Ulrich, 1997). In India too, the research has been on the HR practices and firm performance framework (Kandula, 2002; Singh, 2003a, 2003b), while Agarwala (2003) focuses on innovative HR practices and organizational commitment. There is a need to pursue this line of research and to first establish the existence of the roles and then investigate whether they add value or not. The status of these roles was the focus of recent research studies, which are sparse, such as that of Bahl (2002), Bhandarker (2003) and Bhatnagar and Sharma (2002, 2003a, 2003b). Let us examine the need for this study in an Indian context.

Hypothesis Testing

The Chi-Square test is thought to be appropriate to test the hypothesis as the data was in discrete categorical form. The Chi-Square test is an important test amongst the several tests of significance developed by statistician. Chi-Square symbolically written as $\chi 2$ is a statistical measure used in the context of sampling analysis for comparing the variance to a theoretical variance. As a non-parametric test, it can be used to determine if categorical data shows dependency or the two classifications are independent. It can also be used to make a comparison between theoretical populations and actual data when categories are used. Thus, the Chi-Square test is applicable in large number of problems. The test is, in fact, a technique through the use of which it is possible for researcher to test the significance of association between two variables.

Test Statistics: As variable V_1 and V_2 were discrete categorical variables, Chi-Square test was thought to be the most appropriate test.

Chi-Square Test	Value	df	Asymp. Sig. (2-sided)
Pearson Chi-Square	1.779	2	0.411
N of Valid Cases	120		

Observation: Chi-Square value 1.779 with two degree of freedom with p value of 0.411.

Inference: As p value is greater than 0.05, Ho is accepted. V_1 and V_2 are not dependent.

Findings

This section presents the results of the estimation of our empirical models, starting with the simple binary probity estimation, followed by recursive vicariate probity results. First, as a baseline comparison, we estimate simple univariate probity of the probability of being an entrepreneur (i.e., business owner) at the time of the survey and include a dummy for being returnee but we do not control for the migration decision. The marginal ejects are reported in Table 3.1. We find that returnees are more likely than non-migrants (11 percent) to become entrepreneurs.

Overall, our results suggest that social networks have no significant impact on becoming entrepreneurs for returnees but matter for non-migrants. We also find that human capital and savings matter for becoming entrepreneur for returnees. The joint probability of being a returnee and entrepreneur is around 19 percent and only 14 percent for being a non-migrant and an entrepreneur. Interestingly, conditional on being a returnee, the probability of becoming an entrepreneur is almost 50 percent. This suggests that one needs to control for the endogeneity of temporary migration when studying the entrepreneurship decision (Table 3.2).

The highest correlation is for sensitivity to people potential and needs and the business partner role (.44), while concern for development of capabilities and employee champion role indicate a correlation of .42, and sensitivity to people potential and needs and strategic partner role shows a correlation value of .42. This indicates that development of capabilities and potential development is an activity, which managers correlate highly to the strategic migration to make them rural entrepreneurial, strategic partner and overall business partner role.

Table 3.1: Sample Descriptive Statistics

Variable	Returnees		Non-Migrants	
	Mean	Std. Dev.	Mean	Std. Dev.
Individual Characteristics				
Entrepreneur (percent)	35.43	47.90	30.44	46.02
Age (years)	42.99	7.86	45.65	10.39
Married (percent)	96.57	18.22	95.66	20.37
Educational Level (percent)				
None	14.00	34.75	25.28	43.47
Read and write	9.14	28.86	14.78	35.50
Less than intermediate	15.71	36.45	18.71	39.01
Intermediate	31.14	46.37	18.46	38.80
Higher than intermediate	6.29	24.31	6.18	24.09
University	23.71	42.59	16.59	37.20
Previous Work/Residence Characteristics (percent)				
Urban resident: Previous	65.71	47.53	67.75	46.75
Waged worker : Previous	21.71	41.29	38.39	48.64
Public sector worker: Previous	7.14	25.79	5.63	23.06
Previous Occupation Dummies (percent)				
Technical and scientific: Previous	18.86	39.17	17.41	37.92
Management : Previous	0.57	7.55	2.22	14.72
Clerical: Previous	6.29	24.31	9.91	29.88
Sales: Previous	6.00	23.78	9.81	29.75
Services: Previous	4.86	21.53	6.99	25.51
Agriculture: Previous	10.86	31.15	20.57	40.43
Production: Previous	25.43	43.61	30.19	45.92
Regions of Residence in 1998 (percent)				
Greater Cairo	19.71	39.84	20.60	40.45
Alex and Canal Cities	13.71	34.45	13.32	33.99
Lower Urban	17.43	37.99	16.46	37.08
Upper Urban	14.57	35.33	17.15	37.70
Lower Rural	22.29	41.68	19.40	39.55
Upper Rural	12.29	32.87	13.07	33.71
Sample Size		350		3160

Table 3.2: Further Sensitivity Analysis: Probability of Being an Entrepreneur

	1	2	3	4	5
Returnee	1.312	1.452	1.393	1.366	0.976
	(3.81)**	(4.54)**	(4.29)**	(4.22)**	(1.84)+
Social Networks					
Household size	0.058	0.055	0.054	0.050	0.089
	(4.85)**	(4.87)**	(4.65)**	(4.31)**	(4.88)**
Household size*returnee	-0.077	-0.089	-0.076	-0.076	-0.097
	(2.03)*	(2.41)*	(2.07)*	(2.10)*	(1.61)
Family migrated	-0.040	-0.016	-0.003	0.019	0.128
	(0.21)	(0.09)	(0.02)	(0.10)	(0.56)
Live in rural areas	0.159	0.140	0.153	0.138	0.105
	(2.84)**	(2.63)**	(2.81)**	(2.52)*	(1.40)
Live in village/small town* returnee	-0.029	0.027	-0.006	0.012	0.024
	(0.19)	(0.18)	(0.04)	(0.08)	
Live in Greater Cairo				-0.180	
				(2.51)*	
Live in Greater Cairo* returnee				0.081	
				(0.40)	
Returned in last year	-0.226	-0.120		-0.266	
	(0.58)	(0.33)		(0.69)	
Returned in last 2 years			-0.257		
			(0.87)		
Human Capital					
Migration duration	0.033	0.037	0.037	0.038	0.027
	(2.07)*	(2.33)*	(2.38)*	(2.35)*	(1.08)
Physical Capital					
Migrant used savings				0.031	
				(21.69)**	
Date Started Business				included	

Notes: Robust ‘t’ statistics in parentheses; + significant at 10 percent; * significant at 5 percent; ** significant at 1 percent.

Conclusion

This paper is a first attempt to better understand rural entrepreneurship by combining individual people's migration, human capital, social capital and family background. The recent survey on alumni of Iowa State University used in our paper makes it feasible for us to study the behaviours of rural entrepreneurs. We find that entrepreneurs from rural origins tend to choose to start their businesses in rural areas. Social capital and social networks established in one's home region are shown to be a strong factor in location choice of entrepreneurs. Half of entrepreneurs migrate back to their home state after graduation from ISU, likely to take advantage of local networks or to due to familiarity with local comparative advantages. Rural entrepreneurs are also more likely to obtain financial support from family members, friends and local banks to start a business, which can compensate for their relatively lower earnings/savings.

Consistent with previous literature, we find that family background, specifically parental business experiences, are relevant to self-employment decisions. However, individuals do not necessarily start businesses in rural areas simply because their parents had a farm. Other factors, such as type of business and fields of entrepreneurs' expertise are also important factors.

Our findings suggest a link between rural entrepreneurship and rural brain drain that to date has been overlooked. We find that college-educated entrepreneurs are less likely to migrate to urban areas than are their peers who choose to work for someone else. This may be due in part to established social networks and entrepreneurial role models which makes it easier to start businesses locally. While brain drain policies have tended to focus on providing college scholarships to increase the supply of educated workers, our findings suggest that an important complement to these strategies may involve post-graduation policies to help graduates use their education to create businesses, particularly in their home regions. Given the relatively few job opportunities for college graduates in rural areas, entrepreneurship opportunities provide a potential alternative that not only benefits the individual, but also the larger community. Entrepreneurs can create jobs, increase residents' income and attract financial, technological and human resources to rural communities, all factors which are required for igniting regional growth in the long run.

References

Blanchflower, D. and A. Oswald (2010), "What Makes an Entrepreneur?", *Journal of Labour Economics*, 16, 26-60.

Calv′o-Armengol, A. and Jackson, M.O. (2004), "Social Networks in Determining Employment: Patterns, Dynamics, and Inequality", *American Economic Review*, 94, 426-454.

Coleman, J.S. (1988), "Social Capital in the Creation of Human Capital", *American Journal of Sociology*, 94, S95-S120.

Dustmann, C. and O. Kirchkamp (2006), "The Optimal Migration Duration and Activity Choice after Remigration", *Journal of Development Economics*, 67, 351-72.

Evans, D. and B. Jovanovic (2012), "An Estimated Model of Entrepreneurial Choice under Liquidity Constraints", *Journal of Political Economy*, 97, 808-27.

Evans, D. and L. Leighton (2013), "Some Empirical Aspects of Entrepreneurship", *American Economic Review*, 79, 519-535.

Fischer, C. (2011), "The Urban Experience", New York: Harcourt Brace Jovanovich.

Fischer, C. (2013), "To Dwell Among Friends: Personal Networks in Town and City", Chicago: University of Chicago Press.

Fonseca, R., Lopez-Garcia, P. and C.A. Pissarides (2001), "Entrepreneurship, Start-up Costs and Employment", *European Economic Review*, 45, 692-705.

Girgis, M. (2002), "Would Nationals and Asians Replace Arab Workers in the GCC?", paper presented at the Fourth Mediterranean Forum.

Greve, A. and J. Sala (2003), "Social Networks and Entrepreneurship", Entrepreneurship Theory and Practice, 28, 1-22.

Greene, W. (2013), "Gender Economics Courses in Liberal Arts Colleges: Further Results", *Journal of Economic Education*, 29,

291-300.

Greene, W. (2013), "Econometric Analysis", 5th edition, Upper Saddle River, NJ: Prentice Hall.

Ilahi, N. (2002), "Return Migration and Occupational Change", *Review of Development Economics*, 3, 170-186.

Landes, D. (2006), "The Wealth and Poverty of Nations", New York: W.W. Norton.

Lucas, R.E.B. (2008), "International Migration and Economic Development: Lessons from Low Income Countries", New York: Edward Elgar Publishing.

Massey, D. (2011), "Social Structure, Household Strategies, and the Cumulative Causation of Migration", *Population Index*, 56, 3-26.

McCormick, B. and J. Wahba (2001), "Overseas Work Experience, Savings and Entrepreneurship amongst Returnees to LDCs", *Scottish Journal of Political Economy*, 48, 164-178.

McKenzie, D. and H. Rapoport (2009), "Self-selection Patterns in US-Mexico Migration: The Role of Migration Networks", *Review of Economics and Statistics*.

Mesnard, A. (2004), "Temporary Migration and Capital Market Imperfections", Oxford Economic Papers, 56, 242-262.

Mesnard, A. and M. Ravallion (2006), "The Wealth on New Business Start-ups in a Developing Economy", *Economica*, 73, 367-392.

Mortensen, D.T. and C.A. Pissarides (2013), "New Developments in Models of Search in the Labour Market", in D. Card and O. Ashenfelter (eds.), Handbook of Labour Economics, Amsterdam: Elsevier Science, 2567-2627.

Munshi, K. (2003), "Networks in the Modern Economy: Mexican Migrants in the US Labour Market", *Quarterly Journal of Economics*, 118, 549-599.

Pissarides, C.A. (2000), "Equilibrium Unemployment Theory", second edition, Cambridge, MA: MIT Press.

Putnam, R.D. (2009), "Making Democracy Work: Civic Traditions in Modern Italy", Princeton: Princeton University Press.

Putnam, R.D. (2012), "Bowling Alone", New York: Simon and Schuster.

Schumpeter (1934), "The Theory of Economic Development", Cambridge MA: Harvard University Press (originally published in 1911 in German).

Wahba, J. and Y. Zenou (2005), "Density, Social Networks and Job Search Methods: Theory and Applications to Egypt", *Journal of Development Economics*, 78, 443-473.

Wilde J. (2000), "Identification of Multiple Equation Probit Models with Endogenous Dummy Regressors", *Economics Letters*, 69, 309-312.

Wirth, L. (1938), "Urbanism as a Way of life", *American Journal of Sociology*, 44, 1-24.

4

Supply Chain Management for Rural Women Entrepreneurs

Kuntal Chakrabartty

Introduction

Supply chain management of farming activities in rural India is often disadvantageous for marginal farmers. They produce and sell very small surplus. The striking incident is that, the middlemen, buy most of the surplus from the farmers at very low prices, resulting in lower profit margins on production that barely allow for survival. Lack of preservation units for storage and a wide network of suppliers force the marginal farmers to sell their small surplus into the hands of middlemen at a very low price.

Self Employed Women's Association (SEWA) is a well known organization which has been working for improvement of women's livelihood in India. Since 1972, it has been helping the women, either in the form of marginal producer or entrepreneur all over the country through their various efforts including social network building, financial inclusion and community empowerment through radio. The ultimate goal of SEWA is to provide full employment. RUDI, a multi-trading company aims to generate funds internal to SEWA network that would enhance the quality, capacity and efficiency of rural production. SEWA projected the RUDI initiative in the Sabarkantha district of Gujarat for helping the local skilled businesswomen along the rural production value chain.

Objectives of Rural Entrepreneurship Development

The main objective of rural entrepreneurship development is to reduce poverty with a focus of rural development and gender equality. The link between poverty and growth is employment. The volume of employment is very significant both for an individual and for the society.

SEWA aims for full employment and self-reliance. Concept of full employment is defined as employment that ensures food security, income security and social security at the household level (Ela R. Bhatt).

A majority of the women in rural areas are working as home-based producers. They are also engaged in manufacturing as contact labour, petty vendors/hawkers and casual workers.

The women earn less than their men counterparts within the same sector. This is due to gender base discrimination and segregation.

Removal of this discrimination would have positive effect on women employment and income.

In order to achieve the goals, SEWA focuses on:

1. Promotion of productivity of rural women entrepreneurs.
2. Access to market and capital.
3. Getting rid of middlemen for a better economic situation for the producers.
4. Better terms of trade.
5. More effective organization and managerial capacities.
6. Better qualities of local agro-commodities.
7. Development of the policy advocacy and the collective self-help capacities of rural women entrepreneurs.

To reach the above goals, the programme aims to:

1. Assist in all levels of supply chain—crop production, purchasing, quality control, accounting, processing, brand production and marketing.
2. Connect local SEWA members through value chain linkage.

Following their parent organization's vision of Gandhiji's 'Gram Swaraj', RUDI-SEWA engages to improve the conditions of India's rural women producers by making them self-sufficient.

SEWA Gram Mahila Haat (SGMH): Support Services and Market Opportunities for Rural Women Producers

The SEWA Gram Mahila Haat (SGMH) was created in 1999 as a SEWA sister organization, with the support of Government of Gujarat. The main objective of the organization is to enable rural women producers to have a regular income by providing market related and technical support and identifying local, national and international marketing opportunities. The SEWA Gram Mahila Haat facilitates linkages with market and private companies for 10,000 producers' groups in nine districts across four value chains: agricultural products, handicrafts, spices and forest products.

Most of the rural women producers faced several constraints in accessing markets. SEWA provides support for:

1. Marketing facilities and services (information about current and future prices).
2. Managerial and technical support services to become entrepreneurs/owners of collective enterprises.
3. Working capital assistance.

RUDI: A Rural Distribution Network System

The idea of setting up the Rural Distribution Network is to internally rotate the scarce funds of rural producers in a way that fetches maximum benefit and brings about positive changes in their lives and to provide multi-user facilities, reduce incidental expanses and build up an integrated value chain in order to enhance the efficiency of agricultural activities to reduce the hardships of the producers and to create multiple employment opportunities and an efficient supply of agro-products to rural members.

Working Model of RUDI: RUDI was initiated in 2004 and was officially incorporated in 2007 as a part of SEWA's overall strategy to support the local or 'village economy' by enabling small-scale farmers to sell their product at a fair price so that rural consumers have access to good quality products.

RUDI works with SEWA district associations to link different groups along with the value chain and generate gains for rural producer groups, processors, buyers and retailers. A targeted 80 percent of the total production is stored, cleared and packaged at village hubs. Lastly, it is sent to a district hub which is supplied to the sellers as per the demand.

There are five RUDI processing centres which cover 14 districts of Gujarat. Each processing centre has team with six wings that facilitates the following post-harvest management activities:

1. **Procurement of Agro Products:** SEWA district association procures agro products directly from SEWA farmers' group. It reduces the interference of middlemen, enabling small producers to get the best price for their produce. The women become familiar with price discrepancies between supply and demand and also learn how to determine fair pricing.
2. **Processing and Packaging:** Collected products are then moved into the district RUDI centres. Rural women are taught to clean, sieve, grind, weigh, package and level agro commodities. At this stage, the women producers learn the 'value added' concept as they become witness to the transformation of raw materials to a marketable product.
3. **Quality Control:** Products are also checked to assure quality. In this stage, the rural women learn about the meaning of product quality.
4. **Brand Promotion:** Rural women are also engaged for campaigning of RUDI products. They also learn the importance of spreading awareness of brand at this stage.
5. **Marketing:** RUDI saleswomen or RUDIbens, then buy the goods from the processing centre and sell directly to households in the villages through promotional activities or to other women retailers in the villages. There are around 100 RUDIben who are engaged to market RUDI products. RUDIben earn a 10 percent commission on any product they sell. The products ensure good quality as they

are developed at local level by known rural women.

6. **Record Keeping and Accounting:** Some women members of SEWA-RUDI are trained in basic financial accounting to keep records of the transactions.

Value Chain Linking SEWA Members to the Market

Agricultural value chain can be defined as the full range of activities required to bring a product to final consumers passing through different stages of production, processing and delivery. It can also be defined as market-focused collaboration among different stakeholders who produce and market value added products.

Access to market and distribution of risks and gains along different steps of agricultural value chains varies across the following factors:

1. Gender of producers.
2. Processors (access to processing, technology and information).
3. Market agents (access to transport, safe market place, risk of sexual harassment and abuse).
4. Economies of scale (bringing women together to improve their market position).

SEWA-RUDI value chain network replaced the traditional marketing channels by creating coordination links among farmers, processors, retailers and others. SEWA effort is a landmark of how to include different agents in the value chain, including women—applying a balanced approach that takes into account both competitiveness and equity issues.

ICT in Commercial Supply Chain

Modern information and communication technologies (ICTs) and their applications significantly affect small holders' inclusion in commercial supply chains. ICT application (hardware and software), guided by the business logic, can foster small holders' inclusion by making the following interventions in the supply chain: reducing cost of coordination, (collection of product, distribution of input and so on); increasing transparency in decision-making between partners; reducing transport costs; disseminating market demand and price information; disseminating weather, pest and risk management information; disseminating best practice to meet quality and certification of standards and collecting management data from the field and ensuring traceability.

Inclusive Innovation: Mobile ICT for Rural India

Opportunity of use of appropriate and relevant technologies is an important aspect of inclusiveness. Inclusive innovation also includes the development, diffusion and outreach of innovations that improves the conditions of less advantageous groups other than the poor. The notion of inclusiveness is important, in particular, of gender, where policy makers face the critical task of facilitating women access to technologies which improves their livelihood and opportunity.

An example of inclusive innovation that considers the development of mobile application to strengthen the entrepreneurial capacities of rural women in India is currently being carried out by the Government of Gujarat in collaboration with the Cherie Blair Foundation and Vodafone.

Mobile Base Management

The mobile base management and information system (MIS) is a tool equivalent of an enterprise resource planning software for small entrepreneurs. Running only basic mobile phone and an SMS platform work, it has the potential to unlock huge efficiency gains for small supply chains and transform rural economies.

The Foundation, working in partnership with India's Self Employed Women's Association (SEWA) and with generous support from the Vodafone Foundation in India, has developed RUDI Sandesha Vyavhar (RSV)—a mobile-based management information system (MIS) for SEWA's Rural Distribution Network (RUDI). Operating largely in India's

Gujarat state, RUDI procures farm produce from marginal farmers at market prices, then processes and packages the produce before selling it at affordable prices through their network of saleswomen (RUDIbens). RUDI's reach and scale has increased dramatically, exposing the challenges of paper-based inventory management and sales reporting.

The MIS solution is a simple, user-friendly application targeted at 2,500 women entrepreneurs forming the RUDI network who are also benefiting from broader business development and financial literacy training over the life of the three year-project. RUDIbens can capture sales and place orders for additional stock via SMS using their simple feature phones enabled by a java-based interface. Data is captured on a central database providing information for RUDI's managerial, financial and audit requirements. RUDIbens are also able to generate simple reports on their handset, which gives them essential information for running their businesses. The application is being rolled out to Rudibens through various marketing and training activities, which offer capacity building and long-term enterprise development in addition to the MIS training.

The project aims to reach 2,500 women by 2015 and increase overall RUDI sales by 25 percent. Since the application was first launched in December 2012, RUDIbens have reported significant increase in their monthly sales, and in some cases up to four times as much. Following the monitoring and evaluation of this project, there is potential for it to be scaled into neighbouring states and other SEWA networks.

Benefits of MIS of SEWA-RUDI Network

The benefits of this project should include reduced time and travel cost, as well as efficiency gains in processing time, which translates into higher income and increases the time available for women to devote to other activities, such as developing their business and taking care of their families. Women will avoid trips to warehouse by placing their orders through the mobile services. After their orders are placed, they are packed and distributed to the women in villages.

Limitations to SEWA-RUDI Supply Chain Solution

It is no denying the fact that increasing recognition from local, national and at international level describes the success story of SEWA supply chain management model. Women learn that their work is valuable and that they have the right voice and capacity to lift their family from the trap of poverty. The following factors contribute to SEWA's efficiency, inclusion, expansion and sustainability:

1. Outstanding capacity to organize women and communities and create network of organizations at the bottom level.
2. An organizational model based on values, a strong sense of ownership and a large base of committed women leaders.
3. A realistic and dynamic approach, expanding with available resources and information.

SEWA gives women the tools to become leaders and entrepreneurs and to decide about their own future. Every activity includes capacity building and training of leaders at the grassroots levels. As entrepreneurs, women learn to manage and control their own groups and cooperatives. They learn how to save money, strive for financial sustainability, express their needs and make decisions based on their capacity. In addition, SEWA builds the capacity of poor and illiterate women to engage and reach the highest levels of leadership in the organization. In this process, women build their self-esteem; they are aware that poverty is not a fate; and they receive the knowledge, capacity and resources to act.

SEWA's success model may not generalize to other rural entrepreneurial organizations due to following features:

1. **A Wide Scope that includes all Informal Activities:** SEWA includes all rural women producers in the informal sector. This inclusive network of its members creates a wide range of jobs, both in rural and urban settings. This

makes SEWA uniquely different from any other activity focused organization.

2. **Potential to Create Value Chain among Women:** SEWA's access to greater women in a high population country like India is a source of strength in its ability to reach financial self-reliance. Organizations with same goals in a less populous country may face limited potential membership.
3. **Focus on Women:** SEWA is a woman managed organization. SEWA believes that women have to take lead role to eradicate poverty. They take a lead role because they are resilient, hardworking, and will sustain the family under all circumstances. SEWA creates a space for rural women to build self-confidence and take their own decisions about the matter such as which crop to produce and how to use their earning and savings. It is seen that in a male dominated society, men tend to take over when the business becomes profitable. However, in many countries, women-based organizations failed to totally exclude men. They feel that it may require either joining men's organizations or operating with mixed membership to breakdown social resistance to women only organizations.

Conclusion

It is proven that SEWA-RUDI network has successfully incorporated small women producers in agricultural value chain and has been nurturing livelihood at all levels of rural supply chain. Services like micro credit facilities, rural distribution network, providing training in agriculture processing and incorporating them in mobile base management and information systems (MIS) are now helping many rural women to start and develop small social businesses. The women producers have now become more professional. SEWA's efforts have enabled them to become entrepreneurs and take market opportunities worldwide. RUDIben is unique in that it supports skill enhancement along with employment and therefore builds a platform of inclusive income growth over time. As workers learn new skills, they are likely to develop and move into more profitable business activities along the value chain.

References

Ahirrao, Jitendra (2013), "Entrepreneurship and Rural Women in India", New Century Publications, New Delhi.

Barrett, C.B., M.E. Bachke, M.F. Bellemare, H.C. Michelson, S. Narayanan and T.F. Walker (2010), "Small-holder Participation in Agricultural Value Chain: Comparative Evidence from Three Continents", MPRA Paper, University Library of Munich.

Bhatt, E. (2006), "We are Poor But So Many: The Story of Self-employed Women in India", Oxford University Press, New York.

Chemonics International (2006), "Trade and Investment Programme for Competitive Export Economy (TIPCEE)", Annual Report for Partners, October 2005-September 2006, USAID.

Coulibaly, Y.M., F. Tadjou and E. Baga Yoko (2010), "Strengthening the Position of Women in Agricultural Markets through Collective Action", First research report of OXFAM and Royal Tropical Institute.

Donor Committee for Enterprise Development (2006), "Donor Approaches to Supporting Pro-poor Value Chains.

Ducker, M., and J. Payen (2010), "Information Communication Technology as a Catalyst to Enterprise Competitiveness".

Dymond, A. and S. Esselaar (2010), "Mobile Application for Rural Development", Presentation for Intelecon, December 1, Gender and Rural Employment Policy Brief, FAO.

FAO, IFAD, ILO (2010), "Agricultural Value Chain Development: Threat or Opportunity for Women's Empowerment?", Gender and Rural Employment Policy Brief.

Jhabvala R., S. Desai S. and J. Dave (2009), "Empowering Women in an Insecure World".

Murphy S. (2010), "Changing Perspectives: Small-scale Farmers, Market and Globalization", Hivos Knowledge Programme.

SEWA, "Annual Report, 2012".

SEWA (2009), "Enabling Market Access: SEWA's Effort and Initiatives".

SEWA, "Annual Report, 2010-11".

United States Agency for International Development (2007), "Value Chain Programme Design: Promoting Market Base Solutions for MSME and Industry Competitiveness", USAID, Washington, D.C.

5

Rural Development through Agri-preneurship

Saikat Majumdar and D.C. Kalita

Introduction

Agriculture is the seed bed of Indian Economy. More than half of the national income was contributed by agriculture at the time of Independence. The performance of the agricultural sector influences the growth of Indian economy and still contributes significantly to export earnings and is an important source of raw materials as well as of demand for many industrial products particularly fertilizers, pesticides, agricultural implements and a variety of consumer goods etc. (Bairwa et al., 2014a). It has been the mainstay of the people of our country. In India, about 80 percent of the total population lives in the rural areas. Over 65-70 percent of rural population in India is dependent on agriculture and allied sector for their livelihood and 50 percent of them are poor, and they are not able to satisfy their day to day needs. With the increasing population, rural people are still facing the problem of unemployment. It is a burning problem for rural India, as well as for the country. Agri-preneurship is the solution to many economic problems like poverty and unemployment which are predominant in rural areas. It can be used as a best medicine for solution to these problems in rural areas. Agriculture sector plays an important role in the rural economy of India by providing employment opportunities among the rural people.

Agri-preneurship is defined as generally sustainable, community-oriented, directly marked agriculture. Sustainable agriculture denotes a holistic, system-oriented approach to farming that focuses on the interrelationships of social, economic and environmental processes (Bahal, 2008).

Now, it has become necessary to establish agri-preneurship due to increasing demand for organic and quality food, improvement of livestock business, better production of fruits and vegetables, willingness to enter into the agri-business sector and to reduce malnutrition etc. (Mondal, Ray, 2012).

With this background, an attempt has been made in this paper to study the present status and role of agri-preneurship in India, with the following specific objectives:

- To improve the standard of living of farm households as well as the rural people through agri-preneurship.
- To increase agricultural productivity and profitability for economic stability.

Methodology

The study is mainly based on secondary data regarding recent trends and development of agri-preneurship in India. The secondary data was collected from standard textbooks of related topics, journals and internet. Simple percentages were estimated in the present study. Besides, C.G.R. was also estimated in the present study. The following formula was used to compute the C.G.R.

Where, x is the time variable, y is the variable for which growth rate is calculated and b is the regression co-efficient of y on x. Now, compound growth percentage is

$$(\text{CGR percentage}) = (\text{antilog 'b'} - 1) \times 100$$

The significant of growth rates was tested by applying student 't' test where t = g / SE (r), with (N-2) d. f. where r is the growth and N is the total number of years considered under study.

$$SE(r) = 100\,b / 0.4329 \sqrt{[(\Sigma \log r^2) - (\Sigma \log Y)^2 / N - (\log b)^2 \Sigma x^2] / (N-2)\,\Sigma x2}$$

Result and Discussion

Agri-preneurship in India: In India, a majority of rural population is still dependent upon the agriculture and allied sector for their livelihood. In the stage of unemployment and low growth rate in agriculture sector, it is necessary to create an environment of sustainable agriculture by providing entrepreneurship in agriculture, which is an important pillar of rural development.

In India, agriculture is treated as a family tradition. The farming families—those who are dependent on the agriculture sector—have to realize that it is not only their hobby; it is an important way of earning. Agriculture must be treated as an enterprise with good managerial background for the rural development as well as country's development. Sah (2009) states that developing entrepreneurship in agriculture will solve a host of problems including: (a) reducing the burden of agriculture, (b) generating employment opportunities for rural youth, (c) controlling migration from rural to urban areas, (d) increasing national income, (e) supporting industrial development in rural areas and (f) reducing the pressure on urban cities.

The number of registered agri-preneurship centres in India is presented in Table 5.1. The Table reveals that Tamil Nadu has the highest number of agri-preneurship centres in India. Tamil Nadu was followed by U.P. (13.89 percent), Kerala (9.55 percent), Punjab (8.34 percent), Maharashtra (7.55 percent), Gujarat (6.74 percent), Karnataka (6.65 percent), and M.P. (5.16 percent) respectively.

In India, agri-clinic and agri-business centres got momentum after 2002. The agri-graduates trained were 3,058 in 2002-03 which increased to 3,157 in 2012-13 (Table 5.2). The agri-ventures also increased from 416 in 2002-03 to 990 in 2012-13.

Establishment of Agri-Clinics and Agri-Business Centres: Agri-Clinics and Agri-Business Centre (ACABC) scheme was launched in April 2002 with the objective to supplement the efforts of the Government extension system by facilitating agri-graduates and diploma holders to provide fee-based extension services to farmers. During 2012-13, a subsidy of ₹ 7.64 crore was released for 203 units. Cumulatively, ₹ 18.57 crore was released for 740 units (NABARD Report,

2012-13).

Table 5.1: Number of Registered Units of Agri-preneurship Centres in India

State	Number of Registered Units	Percentage
Tamil Nadu	9,618	16.74
Uttar Pradesh	7,980	13.89
Kerala	5,487	9.55
Punjab	4,791	8.34
Maharashtra	4,339	7.55
Gujarat	3,872	6.74
Karnataka	3,822	6.65
Madhya Pradesh	2,967	5.16
Other States and UTS	14,576	25.37
Total	57,452	100

Source: NABARD Annual Report, 2011.

Table 5.2: Existing Number of Agri-Clinic and Agri-Business Centres in India

Year	Agri-graduates Trained	Agri-ventures Established
2002-03	3,058	416
2003-04	1,110	457
2004-05	2,977	783
2005-06	2,902	1,415
2006-07	3,149	1,081
2007-08	2,742	1,039
2008-09	2,503	824
2009-10	2,564	1,111
2010-11	3,224	1,292
2011-12	4,015	2,139
2012-13 (Till February 28)	3,157	990
C.G.R. (percent)	4.71	10.77

Source: Department of Agriculture and Cooperation, Directorate of Extension, New Delhi.

To improve the standard of living through employment creation has been one of the main objectives of this study. The percentage of persons employed in registered food processing units in India is presented in Table 5.3.

Table 5.3: Persons Employed under Registered Food Processing Units in India

Year	2006-07	2007-08	2008-09	2009-10	2010-11	AAGR
Persons (in lakh)	14.76	15.05	15.64	16.06	16.75	
Growth	6.09	1.96	3.87	2.71	4.3	3.79

Source: Annual Survey of Industries, MOSPI.

Constraints of Agri-preneurship Development in Rural Area: These are as under:

- A good number of rural population in India is dependent on agriculture and allied sector for their livelihood and it is an important way of survival. Due to lack of proper technical knowledge and awareness, it is difficult for farmers to turn their agriculture in to an agri-preneurship.
- In the absence of proper agri-management system farmers are not able to cop up with disasters like heavy rainfall, drought, shortage of fertilizers, pesticides etc. and they lose their interest.
- Lack of awareness and inadequate governmental initiatives would have a negative impact amongst the farmers and their future generations.
- Farmers are reluctant to take the risk of making heavy investments in modern technologies for the business.
- Extension agencies and government bodies should play a more proactive role in promoting agri-preneurship among the villagers.

Strategy for Establishment of Agri-preneurship

- Awareness generation programmes regarding agriculture and its future among the rural people is necessary for promoting a good and successful agri-preneurship.

- Establishment of science and technology entrepreneur parks.
- Active participation of extension agencies and government bodies.
- Promotion of various skill development programmes among the villagers.
- There should be a good network among government officials and farmers about various extension activities.

The benefits for agri-preneurs are given in Table 5.4. The Table reveals that improved cropping pattern was more visible in M.P. as also the cropping intensity.

Employment generation was higher in Manipur (50 percent), followed by Tamil Nadu (36.4 percent), Bihar (33.3), A.P. (30.8 percent), Assam (25 percent) and Karnataka (17.5 percent) respectively.

Conclusion

Rural development is a dynamic process of development of the rural people through various initiatives, so that they can become self-reliant citizens of the country.

Table 5.4: Benefits: As Per Agri-preneurs

(percentages)

State	Improved Cropping Pattern	Cropping Intensity	Income Enhancement	Improved Production Technology
Karnataka	17.5	22.5	40	47.5
Tamil Nadu	27.3	9.1	45.5	54.5
Andhra Pradesh	7.7	23.1	46.2	53.8
Gujarat	0	11.1	11.1	77.8
Maharasthra	0	0	32.7	51
Manipur	12.5	12.5	50	50
Assam	12.5	0	0	0
Odisha	0	0	25	75
Bihar	25	25	37.5	20.8
Madhya Pradesh	66.7	33.3	22.2	33.3
Rajasthan	0	29	51.6	58.1
Uttar Pradesh	25	27.3	70.5	31.8
Overall	**14.4**	**18**	**42.8**	**44.4**

Contd...

State	Productivity Enhancement	Employment Generation	Assistance in Marketing
Karnataka	40	17.5	0
Tamil Nadu	36.4	36.4	0
Andhra Pradesh	30.8	30.8	0
Gujarat	66.7	0	11.1
Maharasthra	49	16.3	2
Manipur	25	50	50
Assam	0	25	0
Odisha	25	0	0
Bihar	16.7	33.3	12.5
Madhya Pradesh	33.3	0	0
Rajasthan	51.6	3.2	0
Uttar Pradesh	25	9.1	4.5
Overall	**36.4**	**16.8**	**4.4**

Source: Global Agri System Private limited Report.

For the development of the rural areas as well as whole country, it is necessary to encourage the rural masses, especially rural youth, to take up initiatives of agri-preneurship as an agri-preneur. There are many areas and sub-areas in agriculture. Within each area, there is a scope for a number of commodities. Based on the needs, agro-climatic conditions and available resources, agri-preneurs can adopt some commodities and flourish on it. There is also much scope for improved production and productivity in agriculture (Mondol and Ray, 2012). Therefore, it is required to train the jobless rural people, graduate youths and others, in agri-business management as agri-preneurs for their betterment as well as for economic stability and for the society's betterment.

References

Acharya, S.S. (2007), "Agribusiness in India: Some Facts and Emerging Issues", *Agricultural Economics Research Review*, Vol. 20 (Conference Issue), pp. 409-424.

"Annual Report, 2006-07", Ministry of Agro and Rural Industries, Government of India.

"Annual Report, 2012-13", Ministry of Micro, Small and Medium Enterprises, Government of India.

"Annual Report, 2012-13", Department of Animal Husbandry,

Dairying and Fisheries, Ministry of Agriculture, Government of India.

Bairwa, S.L. and Kushwaha, S. (2012), "Agro Industry Scenario in India", in S.P. Singh (ed.), Agricultural Research and Sustainable Development in India, Bharti Publications, New Delhi, pp. 159-182.

Bairwa, S.L., Kushwaha, S., Meena, L.K., Lakra, K. and Kumar P. (2014a), "Agribusiness Potential of North Eastern States: A SWOT Analysis", in Singh et al. (ed.), Agribusiness Potentials in India: Experience from Hill States, EBH Publishers (India), Guwahati, pp. 544-556.

Dabson, K. and Markley, D. (2010), "Agripreneurs: A Free Range of Opportunity", Centre for Rural Entrepreneurship.

Entrepreneurship in India (2008), National Knowledge Commission, Government of India.

"National Entrepreneurship Policy", Entrepreneurship Development Institute of India, Ahmedabad, Gujarat.

Planning Commission (2007), Government of India, "Report of the Steering Committee on Agriculture and Allied Sectors for Formulation of the Eleventh Five Year Plan (2007-12)".

Roy, G.L., Mondol, Sagar (2012), "Rural Development, Entrepreneurship and Communication", Kalyani Publications.

Sah, Pooja, Sujan, D.K. and Kashyap, S.K. (2009), "Role of Agripreneurship in the Development of Rural Areas", paper presentation in ICARD at Banaras Hindu University, Varanasi.

"State of Indian Agriculture, 2012-13", Ministry of Agriculture, Department of agriculture and Cooperation, Government of India, New Delhi.

6

Factors Affecting Women Entrepreneurship

Kirankumar Loitongbam and M. Sanjoy Singh

Introduction

Developments in the past few years in Indian economy has witnessed change in the structure of ownership in trade and commerce sector, agriculture sector and the industrial sector. Many entered the world of business of trade and commerce and they have become successful entrepreneurs in various activities. Empowering women, particularly rural women, is a challenge. SHG programmes in rural areas can help to meet these challenges. It will not only enhance productivity and generate employment but would also help to develop economic independence and personal and social capabilities among rural women. Nowadays, economic development is one of the factors that have changed the entire scenario of social and cultural environment within the country, especially for the women. The rural women are engaged in small-scale entrepreneurship programmes with the help of self-help groups. They are economically empowered and are attaining higher status in family and the community. India has emerged as one of the fastest growing economies in the world having recorded an annual growth of more than 7 percent over the last few years. The Government recognizes that in order to sustain its current economic progress, broad based robust growth in industrial and services sector is required.

Many theories of entrepreneurship were framed with many authors emphasizing different factors to explain reasons affecting women entrepreneurship. Those factors include culture (Shapero, 1984), personality (Sexton and Upton, 1990), marginality (Brenner, 1987) and intentionality (Learned,

1995). It has been reported that in general (Zimmerer and Scarborough, 2001), there has been a growing interest and research that has focused on women entrepreneurship. Staw (1991) asserts that experience is the best predictor of business success, especially when the new business is related to earlier business experiences. Entrepreneurs with vast experiences in managing business are more capable of finding ways to open new business compared to employees with different career pathways. Most successful entrepreneurs not only possess certain personal characteristics, they have usually served an apprenticeship within the framework of a small business giving them relevant experience in the big business atmosphere (Timmons, 1994).

Entrepreneurship Development of Rural Women

Entrepreneurial development is one of the significant factors for sustainable socio-economic development. Especially, development of women is inviting special significance because many small and medium firms are well operated through women, though they are less recognized. A self-help group (SHG) is an association of people belonging to similar socio-economic characteristics and residing in same locality. The SHGs are voluntary associations of people formed to attain some common goals. A typical rural women's SHG is a good example of capacity building for a prospective entrepreneur. Its aims include enabling members with no educational or industrial or entrepreneurial background to become self-dependent and self-reliant.

A self-help group is a small economically homogenous and significant group of rural urban poor voluntarily formed to save and mutually agreed to contribute to a common fund to be lent to its members as per group decisions. Scott (2001) identified a number of situations that relate to women's decisions to become entrepreneurs, namely "dynastic compliance", "no other choice", "entrepreneurship by chance", "natural succession", "forced entrepreneurship", "informed entrepreneur" and "pure entrepreneur".

Lerner et al. (1995) have given more importance to start their own businesses (self-fulfilment and personal goal attainment, etc.) as the major reason for women's entrepreneurship.

Shaver et al. (2001) found that entrepreneurs who believed in their skills and ability were motivated to exert the necessary effort. Brindley (2005) cites many research studies that support the argument that men and women view risks differently and that as women become more self-confident, they become less risk averse.

Pattanaik (2003) reveals that SHGs are continuously striving for a better future for rural women as participants, decision-makers and beneficiaries in the domestic, economic, social and cultural spheres of life. Members in SHG agree to save regularly and convert their savings into a common fund and to use this common fund for management and business activities.

SHGs are presently promoted by governments, development banks and voluntary agencies, with focus on social and economic issues, mainly thrift and credit programmes. They are also taking up issues relating to rural industries and modernization of agriculture.

According to Sukhjeet (2006), SHG provides an opportunity for women to improve their financial, social and political status by their involvement as a team. It promotes the quality of life by motivating female human potential. No doubt SHGs will replace commercial or cooperative lending institutions in the villages or at least supplement rural financing.

The concept of self-help group (SHG) is proving to be a helpful instrument for the women empowerment. Participation in income generating activities helps in the overall empowerment of women. The SHGs had a major impact on social and economic life of rural women. It helps women in social recognition of self, status of family in the society and improvement in the standard of living. Higher literacy levels could be helpful for the SHG members to overcome cognitive constraints and to understand government policies, technical understanding and gaining the required skills. Rural women could be motivated to avail finances for starting the entrepreneurial activities. Awareness created about various credit facilities, financial incentives and subsidies through self-help groups is also an important measure.

Statement of Problem

Women in India have been oppressed culturally, socially, economically and politically for centuries. They are exploited at home, in the families, in the society and in the country. In a multi-ethnic and multi-cultural society that exists in India, such exploitation takes various forms. The core of the problem is that they shoulder a number of responsibilities, but they are not given adequate participatory or decision-making power in the family or elsewhere.

Women can gain such power, if their economic, cultural and social status improves. Such type of an overall improvement can be taken care by SHGs. Involvement in self-help groups has enabled women to gain greater control over resources like material possession, intellectual resources like knowledge, information, ideas and decision-making in home, community, society and nation.

Review of Literature

Henry and Kennedy (2002) opined that female entrepreneurship has increased at the global level, in recent times, with a greater number of women setting up businesses and also, self-employed women are increasingly recognised as having an important impact on economy, both as sources of employment and of potential growth. Especially in rural and semi-urban areas, many women are engaged in small and medium scale industries.

Carter and Allen (1997) observed that access to financial

resources and other financial aspects of business had stronger effects on business rather than choice or intention. Stewart et al. (1998) also reported that entrepreneurs were higher in achievement motivation than both corporate managers and small-business owners-managers.

Cromie (1985) found that the need for autonomy and more money were more important motivating factors for women entrepreneurs. It also reported that reasons for women entrepreneurs owning businesses were the formation of initial idea about a product or service, desire for financial independence and the desire to be one's own boss. Anna (2008) in his report, "Women business owners in traditional and non-traditional industries", revealed that traditional women business owners might have different factors that contribute to their success than non-traditional owners. Specifically, for the traditional owners, venture efficacies for opportunity recognition and economic management as well as the career expectation of autonomy and money or wealth, were positively related to sales. For the same group, efficacy towards planning and the need for security were negatively related to sales. For the non-traditional women, venture efficacy towards planning and the career expectation of autonomy were positively related to sales while the expectation of money or wealth was negatively related.

Maas and Herrington (2006) defined push factors as the more negative factors, such as unemployment and retrenchment, which force people to become entrepreneurial in order to survive. They regard pull factors to be the more positive factors, such as government support and role models, which might influence people to choose entrepreneurship as a career option.

Gosh and Cheruvalath (2007) found that only one-fifth of women are drawn into entrepreneurship by pull factors. The rest are forced into entrepreneurship by push factors. Kamal et al. (2000) in their research found that financial support from the government, especially in the start-up capital, is an important factor that motivates women to establish their own businesses. Self-fulfilment, knowledge, skills and experience, including relationship to spouse or father business, are all important factors in the development of women entrepreneurs. Unlike previous research factors such social norms, market network and competition do not seem to be barriers for women in becoming entrepreneurs.

Gosselin and Grise (1990) as cited in Maysami et al. (1999), found that in general, the most common start-up problems seem to be lack of capital. Also important was lack of confidence in female business owners' abilities on the part of banks, suppliers, and clients alike, as well as family issues. Additional problems, such as marketing and labour difficulties and disagreement with associates, may arise after the start-up phase.

Women entrepreneurship is faced with specific obstacles such as family responsibilities, property ownership rights, as well as cultural impediments (Kinyanjui, 2008). Because women are faced with different demands, their motivation to start the business differs from men. For instance, because women have a major responsibility for family and children, it then means that they are prone to start home-based business as well as part-time business.

Various scholars have argued that push and pull factors determine women's disposition to start businesses (Botha, 2006). Push factors are related to negative factors (Maas and Herrington, 2006) and includes unemployment (Hudges, 2006), retrenchment (Hughes, 2006), career frustration (Ghosh and Cheruvalath, 2007), insufficient family income or the need to supplement family income (Segal, et al., 2005), and the need for a flexible work schedule (DeMartino and Barbato, 2002). These factors compel women to become enterprising in order to survive.

Objectives of the Study

1. To know the socio-economic status of women self-help

groups in Thoubal district.
2. To measure the entrepreneurial factor of women SHGs.

Hypothesis of the Study

- H_0: there is no significant difference in income of women SHGs and entrepreneurial factors.
- H_1: there is a significant difference in income of women SHGs and entrepreneurial factors.

The present paper aims to understand the critical study of self-help groups with reference to Thoubal District. This study would be of great help to the implementing agencies to bring necessary improvements in the self-help groups for attaining the overall improvement amongst women.

The knowledge on these aspects could be used to develop strategies to motivate self-help group members for their enhanced participation in the group.

Research Methodology

Data collection method through structured questionnaire was adopted for the study.

Sampling Frame and Data Collection Procedure: On the basis of random sampling, 80 (eighty) women self-help groups promoted by non-governmental agencies were selected in two blocks functioning for at least 3 (three) years at the time of data collection in Thoubal district.

Being descriptive in nature, the study was carried out through a field survey and interview of women in the district. The data used for the study was secondary data comprising of official websites, journals, magazines and articles. The study has made an intensive reference to the primary data for analyzing the above objectives. The data was collected from the selected areas of Thoubal district through questionnaire.

The study has focused on women self-help groups and simple statistical methods like mean, percentage, standard deviation, ranking and ANOVA f-tests have been used as tools of analysis to find out the entrepreneurial factors affecting women self-help groups. The present study covers only women entrepreneurs who were associated with the SHGs.

Data Analysis and Interpretation

Analyses of Demographic Characters for the Women SHGs: Socio-economic status is an important determinant of the livelihoods as it influences levels of knowledge, skill and income conditions which are important for living. Socio-economic status is an economically and sociologically combined total measure of a person's work experience and of family's economic and social position relative to others, based on income, education, and occupation. The household income, earners' education, and occupation are examined as well as combined income, versus that of an individual are assessed. In the present study, the socio-personal characteristics were analysed by using the percentage.

Table 6.1 shows a general profile of women entrepreneurs in the Thoubal District. The respondents were categorised into three distinctive age groups—46.3 percent between 36 and 45 years of age and 31.2 percent above 45 years of age. Only 22.5 percent fell in the age group between 20 and 35.

Educational qualification among women entrepreneurs also highlighted that 41.2 percent of women entrepreneurs were graduates and above, 25.0 percent were educated till higher secondary level, 23.8 percent till the secondary level and 10 percent women entrepreneurs had studied till upper primary.

Types of families of women entrepreneurs revealed that 75.0 percent of women entrepreneurs had separate families while only 25.0 percent had joint families.

The sample covered a wide range of business activity areas with the largest concentration in manufacturing at 60.0 percent, services at 26.2 percent and the rest in wholesale at 13.8 percent.

The same can be said for the firm's legal status with the largest segment as private ventures at 60.0 percent, sole proprietorship at 26.2 percent and the rest as partnerships at 13.8 percent. It was interesting to note that a vast majority of entrepreneurs had experienced an increase in their personal wealth (60.0 percent) since the inception of their businesses. The study shows that 96.0 percent of women entrepreneurs were married. This shows that married women are more involved in entrepreneurial activities.

Table 6.1: Demographic Variables of Women SHGs

S. No.	Indicators	Numbers	Percent
1.	Age group:		
	20-35	18	22.5
	36-45	37	46.3
	46 and above	25	31.2
2.	Education:		
	Graduate and above	33	41.2
	Higher Secondary	20	25.0
	Secondary	19	23.8
	Upper Primary	8	10
3.	Type of family:		
	Nuclear family	60	75
	Joint family	20	25
4.	Firm's main activity:		
	Manufacturer	48	60
	Wholesaler	11	13.8
	Services	21	26.2
5.	Firms legal status:		
	Sole proprietor	21	26.2
	Private	48	60
	Partnership	11	13.8
6.	Personal wealth trend since business inception:		
	Increased	48	60
	Increased significantly	22	27.5
	Remained the same	10	12.5
	Total	80	100

Sources: Survey Data.

Table 6.2 reports the factors affecting women entrepreneurship through, scale of mean, standard deviation and ranking of the sources of economic factors. The inference of the study is that the more the mean value, the more is the level of economic factors experienced. From Table 6.2, it is understood that women entrepreneurs are over-committed to their managerial skills and quite often over worked (mean= 2.98, S.D.=1.13) and was rated as the most important economic factor for women entrepreneurship. The result also points towards raw material as an important economic factor (mean=2.63, S.D.=1.07). The ranking reveals that access to necessary technologies greatly affected the economic factors of the women entrepreneurs (mean=2.36, S.D.=1.12). Satisfaction with the financial access given by the government and other credit institutions (mean= 2.56, S.D.=1.27) was also rated as an important factor affecting women entrepreneurship. The factor of entrepreneurs operating from their own premises (land) to run their business (mean=2.27, S.D.= 1.10) was found negligible.

Table 6.2: Result of the Economic Factors

S. No.	Statements	Mean	Std. Deviation	Ranking
1.	Satisfied with the financial access given by the government and other credit institutions	2.56	1.27	4
2.	I have a better access to market for my products	2.53	1.19	5
3.	I have my own premises (land) to run my business	2.27	1.10	7
4.	I have an access to information to exploit business opportunities	2.50	1.00	6
5.	I have managerial skills	2.98	1.13	1
6.	I have access to necessary technologies	2.36	1.12	3
7.	I have access to necessary raw materials	2.63	1.07	2

Sources: Survey Data.

As seen from Table 6.3, seven items were listed in the

scale to measure the social and cultural factors affecting women entrepreneurship. Most of the entrepreneurs had no cultural influence (mean=3.67, S.D.=0.93). It was also opined that they have better network with outsiders (mean=2.87, S. D.=1.14). The respondents had better social acceptability (mean=2.36, S.D.=1.04) which enabled them to pursue entrepreneurship. Smallest amount of factor that affected social and cultural values comprised of a positive relationship with the workers (mean=1.68, S.D.=0.68).

Table 6.3: Result of the Social and Cultural Factors

S. No.	Statements	Mean	Std. Deviation	Ranking
1.	I have better social acceptability	2.36	1.04	3
2.	I have better contact (network) with outsiders	2.87	1.14	2
3.	I have no prejudice or class bias	2.31	1.13	4
4.	The society' attitude towards my products or services is positive	2.16	1.06	5
5.	I have a positive relationship with the workers	1.68	.68	7
6.	I am not affected by gender inequalities	1.97	.74	6
7.	I have no cultural influence	3.67	.93	1

Sources: Survey Data.

As seen from Table 6.4, seven items were in the scale to measure the legal and administrative factors affecting women entrepreneurship. Most of the entrepreneurs had access to policy makers (mean=3.66, S.D.=0.98). It was followed by the network they had with different administrative bodies (mean=3.46, S.D.=1.11). Least number of respondents found they had no legal, institutional or policy constraints (mean=2.41, S.D.=.79). The interest rate charged by lending institutions that affected legal and administrative value, comprised of a positive relationship with the workers (mean=2.41, S.D.=1.12).

Table 6.4: Legal and Administrative Factors

S. No.	Legal and Administrative Factors	Mean	Std. Deviation	Ranking
1.	I have business assistants and supporters from government bodies	3.1500	1.26391	3
2.	I have a network with different administrative bodies	3.4625	1.11314	2
3.	I have access to policy makers	3.6625	.98010	1
4.	I have no legal, institutional and policy constraints	2.4125	.79067	6
5.	Interest rate charged by lending institutions is reasonable	2.4125	1.12164	6
6.	I have never encountered bureaucracy	2.5750	.92470	4
7.	I am a beneficiary of government incentives	2.4500	1.23144	5

Sources: Survey Data.

To measure the entrepreneurial factors of women SHGs, three items were constructed for this purpose and it was found that among the mean value of the items, economic factors had a large influence i.e. (mean=2.62, S.D.=5.78). For the rest of substance, social and cultural and legal and administrative factors were less significant, i.e. (mean=2.43, S.D.=2.63) and (mean=2.57, S.D.=2.39) respectively. The results show that economic factors had more of an effect on women entrepreneur under SHGs (Table 6.5).

Table 6.6 shows the 'F' test values along with the significance values in entrepreneurial factors. Comparing the 'F' test values and significance values, all the anova comparisons favour the acceptance of null hypothesis. It is to be noted that significance values are below 0.05 for 5 percent level of significance in all the variables except the economic factors, degrees of freedom (4, 75), F=3.17 and significance of 0.18. The hypothesis was rejected that there is a significant difference in income of women SHGs and economic factors. The others two factors (social and cultural and legal and administrative) were accepted—there was no significant difference in income of women SHGs and economic factors, i.e. F (4,75)=0.539 and 0.462, p>0.05.

Table 6.5: Results for Entrepreneurial Factors of Women SHGs

Statements	N	Mean	Std. Deviation
Economic	80	2.62	5.78
Social and cultural	80	2.43	2.63
Legal and Administrative	80	2.57	2.39

Sources: Survey Data.

Table 6.6: Results of the Anova

Statements		Sum of Squares	df	Mean Square	F	Sig.
Economic Factors	Between Groups	382.29	4	95.5	3.17	.018
	Within Groups	2258.19	75	30.1		
	Total	2640.48	79			
Social and Cultural Factors	Between Groups	15.36	4	3.8	.539	.708
	Within Groups	534.43	75	7.1		
	Total	549.80	79			
Legal and Administrative Factors	Between Groups	10.93	4	2.7	.462	.763
	Within Groups	443.81	75	5.9		
	Total	454.75	79			

Sources: Survey Data.

Conclusions and Suggestions

The self-help group (SHG) strategy is one of the instruments for empowerment of women through economic intervention. SHGs have taken the responsibility to decide on the domestic matters of the members' families. After SHGs had been formed, women took part in organizing activities, participated in group discussions and also arranged SHG activities. There is need to focus on other diversified activities for women beyond farming. Focus should also be given on identification of local resource based and need based activities, both production and services, that can support the type of activities. The fact remains that most of the work done by the women at farm and home is disguised as daily chores. Present study is mainly based on entrepreneurial activities other than routine activities.

SHGs are mainly concerned with the enlistment of the women in the society through social and economic aspects. They lead to provide and bring empowerment to the women. SHGs are emerging as a powerful instrument for poverty alleviation. There should be a continuous attempt to inspire, encourage and motivate women entrepreneurs. The government should introduce entrepreneurial development programmes for women. Finance should be made available to women entrepreneurs at a reduced rate of interest. Hence, providing adequate financial support, guidance to start up small businesses and technical support can uplift their standard of living. It is clear from the study that if women entrepreneurs are given proper guidance and training to enhance the profitability of their enterprises, the future will be bright and prosperous.

References

Anna, L. and Chandler, G. (2008), "Women Business Owners in Traditional and Non-traditional Industries", *Journal of Business Venturing,* 15(6), pp. 279-303.

Botha, M. (2006), "Measuring the Effectiveness of the Women Entrepreneurship Programme, as a Training Intervention on Potential Start-ups and established Women Entrepreneurs in South Africa", Pretoria: University of Pretoria.

Brenner, R. (1987), "National Policy and Entrepreneurship: The Statesman's Dilemma", *Journal of Business Venturing*, 2(2), pp. 95-101.

Brindley, C. (2005), "Barriers to Women Achieving their Entrepreneurial Potential", *Women and Risk*, 11(2), pp. 144-161.

DeMartino, R. and Barbato, R. (2003), "Differences between Women and Men MBA Entrepreneurs: Exploring Family Flexibility and Wealth Creation as Career Motivators", *Journal of Business Venturing,* 18(6), pp. 815-832.

Ghosh, P. & Cheruvalath, R. (2007), "Indian Female Entrepreneurs as Catalysts for Economic Growth and Development", *The International Journal of Entrepreneurship and Innovations,* 8(2), pp. 139-148.

Gosselin, L. and Grise as cited in Maysami, Cooper et al., (1999), "Female Business Owners in Singapore and Elsewhere: A Review of Studies", *Journal of Small Business Management,* 37(1).

Heilman, M.E. and Chen, J.J. (2003), "Entrepreneurship as a Solution: The Allure of Self-employment for Women and Minorities", *Human Resources Management Review,* 13(2), pp. 347-364.

Kinyanjui, M.N. (2008), "From Home to Jua Kali Enterprise Spaces: Entrepreneurs and Female Gender Identity", *International Journal of Entrepreneurship and Small Business,* 5(3-4), pp. 401-411.

Lerner, M. and Brush, C.G. (1995), "Factors Affecting Performance of Israeli Women Entrepreneurs: An Examination of Alternative Perspectives", Boston MA: Babson College.

Maas, G. and Herrington, M. (2006), "Global Entrepreneurship Monitor (GEM): South Africa Report", Cape Town: University of Cape Town.

Pattanaik, Sunanda and Smaranika (2003), "Empowerment through SHG: A Case Study of Gajapati District", *International Journal of Research in Commerce & Management*, 1(8).

Scott, C.E. (2001), "Why More Women Are Becoming Entrepreneurs", *Journal of Small Business Management,* 24(4), pp. 37-44.

Segal, G. and Borgia, D. (2005), "The Motivation To Become An Entrepreneur", *International Journal of Entrepreneurial Behaviour and Research,* 11(1), pp. 42-57.

Sexton, D.L. and Upton, N.B (1990), "Female and Male Entrepreneurs: Psychological Characteristics", *Journal of Business Venturing*, 5, pp. 29-36.

Shapero, A. (1984), "The Entrepreneurial Event", in C. Kent (ed.), The Environment for Entrepreneurship, Lexington, D.C. Heath, pp. 21-40.

Sukhjeet, K. (2006), "Development of Entrepreneurship among Rural Women", *Journal of Social Science,* 13(2), pp. 147-149.

Zimmerer, T.W. and Scarborough, N.M. (2001), "Essentials of Entrepreneurship and Small Business Management", Upper Saddle River, NJ: Prentice Hall.

7

Horticulture Entrepreneurship

C.P. Suresh, Kalkame Ch. Momin, Y.S. Singh and Chelsea Ch.Momin

Introduction

The North-Eastern region of India has been considered to be the richest reservoir of genetic variability of horticultural crops including fruits, vegetables, flowers, plantation crops, spices, medicinal and aromatic plants. The North-East region lies between 21.5° N-29.5°N latitudes and 85.5°E-97.3°E longitudes and comprises of eight states, viz. Assam, Arunachal Pradesh, Meghalaya, Manipur, Mizoram, Nagaland, Tripura and Sikkim. Horticulture sector has made tremendous progress in terms of expansion in area and production under different crops, diversification, technological interventions for production and post-harvest and forward linkages through value addition and marketing. It may be mentioned that in hill areas particularly, horticultural crops cultivation as an alternative to jhuming may prove to be a boon for the regional economy. In North-East region, farming being the main income of the people, development of horticulture will markedly improve the economy and livelihood of the people.

In India, the Department of Agriculture and Cooperation, Ministry of Agriculture, is the nodal agency for promoting entrepreneurial activities in horticulture sector of the country. Its focus is on unleashing the advantages of various horticultural crops through its schemes like, National Horticulture Mission and Technology Mission for Integrated Development of Horticulture in North Eastern States, Sikkim, Jammu and Kashmir, Himachal Pradesh and Uttarakhand.

National Horticulture Board (NHB) has also been set up to promote integrated development in horticulture as well as for coordinating, stimulating and sustaining the production and processing of fruits and vegetables.

Initiative has also been taken up to promote modern 'terminal markets' for fruits, vegetables and other perishables in important urban centres of the country to provide the state-of-the-art infrastructure facilities for electronic auction, cold chain and logistics, etc.

Such market seeks to allow easy access to farmers for the marketing of their produce. Hence, there exists innumerable business opportunities in the horticulture sector of India and in particular, the North-East India which has a rich diversity of flora and fauna. Investors and entrepreneurs, from all over the world, are making greater investments into the sector and are actively involved in trading of horticultural crops.

Status of Horticulture in North-East India

The North-East (NE) region is characterized by difficult terrain, wide variability in slope and altitude, land tenure system and traditional cultivation practices. The approximate area under horticulture in the region was around 1,299.80 thousand hectares with a production of 10,694.90 thousand MT (NHB database, 2013). The area under flowers and medicinal plants is still negligible; which is an emerging sector in the region. Assam is the leading state in the NE region which has the maximum area and production under horticultural crops and is followed by Tripura. The area, production and productivity of major horticultural crops like fruits, vegetables, spices and plantation crops have been presented in Table 7.1.

The transport and communication system is a major drawback in the region and majority of the places still remain inaccessible. Majority of the population is dependent on agriculture, horticulture and allied land based activities. Agriculture is mostly rainfed, monocropped and at subsistence level.

Table 7.1: Area, Production and Productivity of Major Horticultural Crops in North-East India

Crops	Physical Terms	Assam	Meghalaya	Nagaland	Tripura
Fruits	Area	150.7	33.2	37.2	60.1
	Production	2073.8	316.6	276.0	697.9
	Productivity	13.8	9.5	7.4	11.6
Vegetables	Area	278.7	40.5	26.0	45.1
	Production	3415.1	403.4	207.7	754.1
	Productivity	12.3	10.0	8.0	16.7
Spices	Area	96.7	16.9	9.8	5.7
	Production	287.5	74.8	39.2	18.0
	Productivity	3.0	4.4	4.0	3.2
Plantation	Area	98.2	23.1	1.5	15.3
	Production	183.40	29.2	10.5	33.5
	Productivity	NA	-	-	-

Contd...

Crops	Physical Terms	Manipur	Sikkim	Mizoram	Arunachal Pradesh
Fruits	Area	51.9	14.7	49.7	86.9
	Production	405.9	24.0	293.0	312.20
	Productivity	8.5	1.6	5.9	3.6
Vegetables	Area	21.7	25.6	39.3	1.5
	Production	219.8	132.5	236.7	37.6
	Productivity	10.1	5.2	6.0	24.7
Spices	Area	10.5	26.6	22.5	10.2
	Production	24.1	60.1	59.6	64.3
	Productivity	2.3	2.3	2.7	6.3
Plantation	Area	-	-	7.6	-
	Production	-	-	4.4	-
	Productivity	-	-	-	-

*Area in 000'ha, Production in 000'MT and Productivity in MT/Ha
Source: NHB, 2013.

The diverse agro-climatic conditions, varied soil type and abundance of rainfall offers immense scope for cultivation of different types of horticultural crops, including fruits, vegetables, flowers, plantation crops, tuber and rhizomatous crops and crops of medicinal and other economic values. The fruits grown in this region range from tropical and sub-tropical fruits like banana, papaya, pineapple and citrus to temperate fruits like apple, pear, peach and plum. Both the indigenous tropical vegetables and temperate vegetables are grown to a considerable extent and the major vegetables grown in the regions include brinjal, cabbage, cauliflower, okra, onion, pea, potato, tomato, knol-khol, radish, carrot, French bean and different cucurbitaceous crops.

It is worth mentioning here that the region is blessed with about 600 different species of orchid like *Dendrobium*, *Cattleya*, *Aerides*, *Phalaenopsis*, *Cymbidium*, *Vanda*, *Phaius*, etc. The other commercial flowers that are grown include marigold, tuberose, gladiolus, carnation, lilium, alstroemeria, rose and chrysanthemum. Tuber and rhizomatous crops like tapioca (cassava), sweet potato, dioscorea, colocasia, ginger and turmeric grow abundantly in the region, while plantation crops like tea have considerable impact on the economy of the Assam region, in particular.

Apart from these, there are certain underutilized or lesser known horticultural crops which are grown at a large scale in some or other parts of the region by tribals. These underutilized crops include passion fruit, cane fruit, aonla, jackfruit, *Myrica spp.*, *Prunus pashia*, chow-chow, parkia, sweet gourd (kakrol), bamboo shoots, etc. These crops are grown in such a large scale that they are not only consumed by tribals/people of the region but are also exported outside the region. A significant increase in area under cultivation has been witnessed in fruits, vegetables, flowers, spices and plantation crops.

Strength of the Region

The North-East India is blessed with a huge diversity of flora and fauna, forest wealth, medicinal and aromatic plants, oil and gas, limestone, coal, etc. and has all the potential to become one of the commercial hubs in the future. The region is closely connected to Bhutan in the North West, China in the North, Bangladesh in the South West and Myanmar in the East which gives an added advantage of becoming an international hub of trade and commerce. The North-Eastern region is characterized by hills and mountains with folded topography, plateaus and hills with near tropical to alpine climatic conditions. The unique diversity in agro-climatic conditions coupled with fertile and well-drained soil makes this region suitable for growing a large number of horticultural crops like wide range of fruits, vegetables and plantation crops. Some of the selected and promising crops of temperate and tropical fruits are grown commercially by some of the farmers in some potential areas. Considering the site, situation and specific problems, gentle hill slope even with shallow soil depths with sufficient soil moisture regime is considered suitable for horticultural crop cultivation. There lies an immense potential for vertical and horizontal growth of horticulture sector in the region.

Horticulture provides the much needed opportunity for diversification in agriculture especially in the context of peculiar topography and agro-climatic conditions of the hill states where the scope for production of conventional field crops is limited. Horticulture development is an effective tool for accelerating development in hilly areas due to limited land available for cultivation, availability of cultivable waste lands and necessity of supplementary jobs and income opportunities. However, large scale policy interventions are required to promote this sector. As regards financial input, lending to plantation and horticulture sector is a challenging task as most of these crops are having long gestation period, perishable in nature and are labour and capital intensive with comparatively higher level of technical inputs. Considering the agro-climatic and socio-economic scenario prevalent in this region, it would be pertinent to concentrate on some important horticultural aspects in the region.

Scope of Horticulture Entrepreneurship

Diversification of agriculture is considered as an important strategy for agricultural development in India and importance of horticultural crops as a means of diversification and creation of additional employment opportunities in rural areas is well accepted. Besides, it also promotes development of agro-industries' with value addition. Although, the North-East region has the potential for development of horticulture with its wide range of topographical and agro-climatic variations, the region is yet to harness the potentiality. Commercially, grown crops usually are high value crops and certain special varieties of horticultural crops can be grown in marginal and degraded soils as well by identifying the suitable species/root stocks. There is immense scope of entrepreneurship in the following fields.

Mushroom Production: In the hill states of North-Eastern region, mushrooms are a popular food and are highly consumed. Though many types of mushrooms are being commercially produced everywhere, the button mushroom (*agaricus bisporus*), oyster (*pleurotus spp.*), paddy straw mushroom (*volvariella volvacea*), milky mushroom (*calocybe indica*) are the most popular with the growers and consumers in the region. Mushroom is a low volume-high value commodity and is a highly suitable agro-industrial venture. Mushrooms are being processed into fresh, dried and pickled forms. It is not only highly profitable but is also labour-intensive, and above all not dependent on arable land. Mushrooms are grown indoors and rooms or huts can be raised on otherwise idle land such as slopes and is highly suited to women folk. Being highly profitable and labour intensive, it can attract the youth. Mushrooms have also a good market in the neighbouring countries as well except may be Bangladesh.

Value Added Products: With changing food habits, the demand for processed and value added products is increasing rapidly. The fruit and vegetable sector has a fundamental role in farm revenue improvement, poverty mitigation, food security and sustainable agriculture. This sector, however, suffers greatly from post-harvest losses. Value addition is a process of increasing the economic value and consumer appeal of a commodity. It is a production/marketing strategy driven by customer needs and preferences. Produce is changed from its original form to a more desirable form like apple pie, jams, jellies, juice, wine and pickles etc.

Fruits and Vegetables: Most fruits and vegetables produced in India are still consumed fresh except for a very small quantity going for the manufacture of various products. The primary reason for processing fruits and vegetables is to extend the shelf life beyond the period when there is plenty into the bend or away of season period. Over the last few years, there has been a positive growth in ready to serve beverages, fruit juices and pulps, dehydrated and frozen fruits and vegetable products, tomato products, pickles, processed mushrooms and curried vegetables. Besides processing of major fruits for various value added products, the processing industries are also looking for value added products from minor or underutilized fruits.

Flowers: Floriculture has emerged as a major diversification option in the agri-business in recent years. The value added products from flowers include dry flowers and pot pourri, essential oils, flavours and fragrances, pharmaceutical and neutraceutical products, pigments and natural dyes, *gulkand*, rose water, vanilla products and insecticidal and nematicidal compounds. Export of value added products like oil rather than the raw material like rose petals, can help generate substantial revenue in international market. The consumption basket is getting diversified towards value-added floral products such as essences, perfumes, and other by-products from flowers. It is important for production to respond to these shifts in consumption. There is a need for value addition in floricultural products through processing, packaging, and supply chain management so that farm incomes expand and employment is generated.

Spices and Plantation Crops: Blessed with suitable agro-climatic conditions, NE region abounds in varieties of spices and plantation crops for processing industries. The region has tremendous potential for further development of processing industries based on locally available materials like tea, cashewnut, rubber, black pepper, garlic, ginger, turmeric, cardamom, cinnamon,etc. The high-priced spice and plantation crops may become a boon for the people of the region. These crops do not require much external input, are low-volume, non-perishable and less labour intensive. These crops also give high economic returns with a higher market price. Generating awareness about the potential of spices and plantation crops would encourage the sustainability of rural systems and improve the quality of life of marginal farmers.

Bamboo Shoot: Bamboo shoots find an important place in the North-East cuisine. It is no longer an "orphan species" or poor men's timber. It is either consumed fresh or processed because of its exotic taste and flavour. Bamboo shoots are low in fats and calories but rich in fibre with about 90 percent water. It is not only popular in the NE region but is also consumed by people staying in metropolitan cities like Mumbai, Kolkata, Delhi, Bangalore, etc. Being a minor or lesser known food product, bamboo shoot processing has a good potential to be developed as an innovative and promising enterprise. Besides being used as a food, there are many other products that can be made from bamboo like bamboo pulp and paper, floor boards, panels, ceiling, landscaping, eco tourism, building furniture etc.

Commercialization of Potential Fruit Crops: NE region has huge potential for commercial cultivation of fruits like banana, pineapple, kiwi, apple, passion fruit, lemon, lime, orange, mandarin, etc. There is enough scope for increasing farm returns and productivity through the adoption of improved package of practices like INM, IPM, good irrigation system, use of quality seeds and planting materials, high density planting etc.

Organic Farming: The North-East, where very little amount of fertilizers and pesticides are used for agriculture, has immense potential for organic farming, agricultural experts and scientists have long pointed out. The region has the potential to carve a niche in the organic foods market once the production, certification and marketing of the produce are institutionalized. There is a need to promote organic farming in production of different horticultural commodities with the objective of promoting exports and improve returns. There is, therefore, an urgent need to develop technology for organic farming and create awareness for the benefits it provides. This calls for standardization of technologies for producing vermi-compost, bio-fertilizer, mycorrhizae and bio-pesticides for different crops. There is also need to develop guidelines for this purpose and designate agency/agencies for accreditation of such produce meeting international requirements.

Development of Processing Industries: For the NE region, the success of fruits and vegetable growing is closely linked with the availability of processing facilities. The processing industry can help to a certain extent in sorting out the problem of proper disposal of perishable commodities. Till today, there are a few number of cold storage facilities available in the whole of North-East region; few processing units exist but are not functioning up to the desired capacity. Use of appropriate pre- and post-harvest practices for horticultural crops is vital for the success of the crops and also to garner good returns. Unfortunately, this is one of the weakest areas in the entire region.

Conclusion

Horticulture provides much needed opportunities for diversification towards high value crops which yield higher income in comparison to traditional crops and thereby improve livelihood security of the farmers in hilly areas where non-farm sources of income are extremely limited. Normally, production and distribution bottlenecks created by deficiencies in roads, telecom, etc., create a drag on growth in the long run. Infrastructure development in the region in terms of connectivity of roads, telecom, etc., is inadequate. This has influenced availability of technology related inputs and marketing and storage facilities for horticultural crops which are mostly perishable in nature.

These factors together affect productivity negatively and reduce returns from cultivation of these crops which in turn influence farmer's decisions in area allocation. However, the entire North-East India has great advantage of agro-climatic diversity for growing a large variety of horticultural crops. This natural advantage should be exploited to the benefit of farmers. Hence, improving infrastructure and removing bottlenecks hindering growth productivity of horticultural crops hold prime importance for achieving the desired levels of horticulture development in the region. Fortunately, solutions are at hand. Resolving the inputs and infrastructure facilities will definitely make the difference in horticultural development not only for the future but even for the present.

References

Ghosh, S.P. (1985), "Horticulture in North Eastern India", *Indian Journal of Hill Farming,* 7: 11-21.

Verma, N.D. and Bhatt, B.P. (2001), "Steps Towards Modernization of Agriculture in NEH Region", Venus Printers and Publishers, New Delhi.

Yadav, R.K., Yadav, D.S., Rai, N, and Patel, K.K. (2013), "Prospects of Horticulture in North Eastern Region", *ENVIS Bulletin: Himalayan Ecology,* 11(2): 1-16.

8

Livestock in the Livelihood of the Tribals

Paul Dayo Passah and B.K. Mishra

Introduction

India has a vast resource of livestock which plays a vital role in promoting the socio-economic welfare of the rural masses. Indian agriculture began by 9000 BC with the cultivation of plants, and thereafter, with the domestication of animals like sheeps and goats. Since then, livestock management has been an important constituent and an integral part of agriculture in India. Until today, mixed crop and livestock farming systems is a form of livestock rearing, practiced by most peasants and farmers across the country. With India moving at par with other developed countries in livestock sector, ranking first in cattle and buffaloes and in milk production, second in goat, third in sheep, fourth in camel and in egg production and fifth in poultry as per FAO, 2003, this industry has opened up new avenues for the many aspiring entrepreneurs who are willing to make changes in the socio-economic status of the country.

The role of livestock in improving the livelihood of the tribals of Meghalaya stands strong today with the availability of exotic breeds, improved technological know-how and other extension activities offered by the animal husbandry and veterinary departments. About 73 percent of the rural population of Meghalaya owns some form of livestock for subsidiary living. With the increase in the demand for meat and milk and other related products in this region, this sector has a great potential for improving the socio-economic conditions and resources of the poor livestock owners to ensure food supply and to reduce poverty. Thus, livestock sector has a great potential of meeting not only the local, national and even the global demands for meat, milk, eggs, and other livestock related products, but it will also help in generating self-employment through livestock entrepreneurship.

Animal Husbandry and Dairying: Indian Scenario

These two sectors contribute about 26 percent of the total output from the agriculture sector. The total livestock population in India as per the 1992 census increased by more than 470 million from 273 million in 1951, an increase of 60.4 percent. Similarly, there was a 31.7 percent growth in cattle and 92.2 percent in buffalo population during 1951-1992. Within the same time period, sheep population increased by 30 percent and that of goats and pigs by 145 percent and 190 percent respectively. According to the 50th National Sample Survey (NSS), the employment in animal husbandry sector was 9.8 million (provisional) in the principal status and another 8.6 million (provisional) in the subsidiary status (Table 8.1). [1]

Today, livestock sector plays a crucial role in helping many of India's rural poor, contributing about 9 percent to GDP and providing employment to 8 percent of the labour force. In recent years, livestock output is rising by about 5 percent a year, higher than that in the agricultural sector. Livestock sector can supply a flow of essential food products, draught power, manure, employment, and income (Table 8.2). The livestock wealth is strongly egalitarian and hence, from the equity and livelihood perspective it is seen as an important component in poverty alleviation programmes. [2]

Livestock Scenario in Meghalaya

Meghalaya, well known as '*the abode of clouds*' has a population of 2,964,007 (2011) covering an area of approximately 300 km. in length and 100 km. in breadth (22,429 sq. km.). Meghalaya is made up of a majority of tribal people. The East Khasi and Jaintia Hills are Nepali belts and is an agricultural area with cattle rearing as the main occupation. Meghalaya is strongly an agrarian economy. Agriculture and other allied activities engage nearly two-thirds of the total workforce in the State. However, in spite of a large crowd involved in agriculture, the State is still dependent on imports from other States for food grains, meat, eggs etc. The incidence of poverty in rural areas is expected to be about 55 percent which is almost double of that in the urban areas. [3]

Table 8.1: Total Livestock and Poultry Population (2003)

(in thousand)

State	Cattle	Sheeps	Goats	Pigs
Meghalaya	767	18	327	419
NEHR	3,048	57	1,379	2,273
India	1,85,181	61,469	1,24,358	13,518

Contd...

State	Horses/Ponies	Total Livestock	Total Poultry
Meghalaya	2	1,533	2,821
NEHR	16	7,043	14,798
India	751	3,85,620	4,89,012

Source: Department of Animal Husbandry and Dairying, Government of India.

Table 8.2: Milk Production in India (Million Tonnes)

2005-06	2006-07	2007-08	2008-09	2009-10	2010-11	2011-12
97.1	102.6	107.9	112.2	116.4	121.8	127.3

Source: Department of Animal Husbandry and Dairying, Government of India.

Meghalaya presently has 11 districts with the major tribal communities being the Khasis, the Jaintias (Pnars) and the Garos. The agricultural operations face a lot of problems today due to the topography, climatic conditions and socio-economic conditions. The returns from livestock sector in small and medium holdings are larger and highly sustainable. Presently, around 2 lakh milch cows and buffalos are spread over 5,000 villages and about 1.64 lakh households are engaged in small animals and ruminants and other allied activities. Added to this, due to social and religious acceptance, the consumption of meat is relatively higher in Meghalaya.

However, that of milk and milk products is lower due to low consumption rate. Livestock population in Meghalaya is dominated by cattle with 6.98 lakh indigenous and 16.8 thousand crossbred cattle. The pig population on the other hand is substantial at 2.94 lakh, with goats at about 1.96 lakh. Poultry comprises about 1.68 lakh desi and 4.5 thousand improved variety. [4] However, the veterinary services in the State are not satisfactory to meet the needs of the livestock sectors existing within the State (Table 8.3).

Table 8.3: Density of Livestock Population per Sq. Kms in Meghalaya [5]

S. No.	District	Cross-bred Cattle	Indigenous Cattle	Buffaloes	Pigs
1.	E. Khasi Hills	1.93	19.22	0.3	31
2.	Ri-Bhoi	2.75	16.52	1.83	7.72
3.	W. Khasi Hills	0.1	17.75	1.23	5.82
4.	Jaintia Hills	0.13	26.09	0.52	9.97
5.	E. Garo Hills	0.4	40.72	1.34	13.96
6.	W. Garo Hills	1.03	54.84	4.07	18.15
7.	S. Garo Hills	0.04	22.64	0.75	9.45
	MEGHALAYA	0.79	28.41	1.5	13.11

Contd...

S. No.	District	Sheeps	Goats	Poultry	
				Fowls	Ducks
1.	E. Khasi Hills	4.17	11.96	69.74	0.51
2.	Ri-Bhoi	0.03	5.46	76.21	1.22
3.	W. Khasi Hills	1.69	8.37	44.38	-
4.	Jaintia Hills	0.02	5.68	54.22	0.49
5.	E. Garo Hills	-	6.65	124.7	4.52
6.	W. Garo Hills	0.07	13.37	131.5	8.19
7.	S. Garo Hills	0.01	10.1	78	1.16
	MEGHALAYA	1.03	8.72	79.16	2.26

Source: Department of Animal Husbandry and Dairying, Government of India.

Together with the traditional meat-eating habit, urbanization and changes in lifestyle, the state is deficit in production of livestock products. The total shortfall is 7.3 thousand tons of beef (total requirement being 28.8 thousand tonnes), 900 tonnes of pork (total consumption being 8,500 tonnes), and 32 million eggs out of the total requirement of 1116.7 million. Consequently, inter-state trade of livestock often becomes the only solution to the increase in the demand for livestock products (Table 8.4). [6]

Table 8.4: Production of Beef and Pork in Meghalaya

Products	Requirement (thousand tonnes)	Deficit (thousand tonnes)
Beef	35.8	12.3
Pork	14.5	5.5

Source: Progress Report of Meghalaya, 2009-10.

Thus, there is an immediate need to find ways and means to bridge the widening gap between the demand and supply of livestock products within the State. In this regard, IFAD (Final Design Report, 2014) has established 120 livestock development centres (LDCs) within the village clusters to support natural resources and food security together with the supportive animal breeding and feeding initiatives.

Livestock Farming Practices in Meghalaya

A major thrust on livestock farming practices as seen in Meghalaya is given to the rearing of cattle, pig and poultry, with little preferences for goat and sheep. These three major livestock has provided the tribals of Meghalaya with subsidiary means to meet their daily requirements in life.

Piggery Development: The State has a sizeable population of pigs comprising about 28.10 percent of the country's total pig population, with pork being the most preferred meat item among the non-vegetarian folk of this area. The number of pigs slaughtered annually during the last four years was estimated at about 1.81 lakh. Pig rearing is a profitable business in all the three major regions due to the suitable climate and the availability of good market with a wide scope for growth and development. Although exotic breeds like the *large yorkshire*, *hampshire*, *landrace*, *duroc*, *tamworth* and *large black* are available, a larger population adopts non-descript indigenous germplasm which often acts as a barrier to the pig industry.

A study made in Garobadha (Garo Hills), shows that about 88 percent of the total villages reared non-descript local breeds and only 10-12 percent reared crossed bred pigs. Besides, pig industry proves to be extremely cost-effective as most of the farmers used traditional methods in carrying out different activities like feeding, housing, health care etc. As for example, 60 percent used *mixed type* of shed, 37 percent used *kutcha* type and only 3 percent used *pucca* houses (ICAR). Lack of superior germplasm, infrastructures like artificial insemination centre and diseases investigation laboratories, non-availability of fodder seed production farms and other extension services greatly act as major constraints in the pig industry (Tables 8.5 and 8.6).

Table 8.5: Breeding Technologies Adoption Level (2003)

Breeding Adopted 10.32 percent		Breeding Not Adopted	Castration	
AI	Natural Service		Adopted	Not Adopted
22.22 percent	77.78 percent	89.68 percent	46.70 percent	53.30 percent

Source: ICAR.

Table 8.6: Adoption of Crossbreds in Meghalaya: 1992 and 2003

State	1992 (percent)			2003 (percent)		
	Cattle	Sheep	Pig	Cattle	Sheep	Pig
Meghalaya	2.4	-	34.6	3.3	3.5	6.8
NER	5.4	5.9	27.9	8.5	2.3	36.9
India	7.4	7.2	14.5	13.7	9.3	16.1

Source: Livestock Census (1992 and 2003), Ministry of Agriculture, Government of India.

Pigs are well acclimatized to NER and the generation

interval is short and prolific in nature. A larger stock provides ample opportunities for proper selection for fattening and breeding purposes. The amount of meat per unit live weight of pig is larger than any other kind of livestock with more energy per unit weight. The by-products like liver, ears, brain, snout, lips, tongue, heart, tail etc. are very much cherished by the local people and therefore will double the source of income of the farmers. A pig farm investment also requires minimum labour but the returns over investments are fast and quicker. This is even doubled with the efficient use of garbage, garden wastes and discarded feeds. Taking into consideration the paucity of protein supply and the rising demand for the same, it is evident that the expansion, growth and development of this sector will assure new hope and better promises to the rising entrepreneurs and farmers of the State (Table 8.7).

Table 8.7: Pig Population in Meghalaya (2007 Census)

S. No.	District	Pigs		Total Pigs
		Crossbred	Indigenous	
1.	East Khasi H	28,671	90,686	1,19,357
2.	Ri-Bhoi	4,044	38,426	42,470
3.	West Khasi H	9,272	76,438	8,5710
4.	Jaintia H	13,776	56,432	70,208
5.	East Garo H	9,466	46,071	55,537
6.	West Garo H	2,152	1,26,194	1,28,346
7.	South Garo H	2,776	19,953	22,729
	State (Overall)	70,157	4,54,200	5,24,357

Source: Animal Husbandry and Veterinary Department, Government of Meghalaya.

Cattle Development: India has the largest cattle population of approximately 300 million in the world. However, the milk output per milch animal is very low as against the world average (Indian average is 1,380 litres against world average of 2,350 litres per animal per year). This industry makes available the essential nutritional benefits and makes a significant contribution to rural and national economies, thus, playing an important role in achieving a sustainable rural development. The Government data shows that the value of output from milk and milk products was ₹ 2,62,215 crore in 2010-11, the highest amongst the livestock products. Milk production is 127 million tons a year, which is beyond that of wheat, rice and pulses. [7] However, the per capita availability is only 230 gm. which is quite low at the world level. In Meghalaya, the yield from crossbred and indigenous cows is 3,245 and 274 kg. per year respectively which could safely be increased to the targeted levels through the input services provided at the farmers' door. Though the dairy industry contributed a lot to the Indian GDP, the industry receives far less government budgeting than the agriculture sector. [8]

As far as meat is concerned, about 80-85 percent of the population of Meghalaya consumes meat. The availability of cattle within the State is less and as such the demands of beef could not be met from within the state. 1.89 lakh cattle were slaughtered during the last four years out of which 40 percent were imported from outside the State. The percent change in population and in composition of crossbred cattle in 2003 over 1983 was 24.04 and 1.85 percent respectively. However, it was found negative (-2.71 percent and -6.060 percent) in indigenous cattle of NER. This decline was due to low milk yields. The adoption of crossbred cattle will help the State to produce more meat and extra income for the farmers.

Looking at the acute availability of meat and milk, as well as that of cold meat which is well accepted and fast developing in the State today, cattle development can prove to be a profitable business in Meghalaya. By-products like kidneys, liver, stomach, ears, brains, skin, snout, lips, gullets, tongue, heart, tail etc. as well as the dung are in high demand in the market. The sales of dairy products like sweets are also gaining great momentum and are highly competitive at the market level. Besides, this sector can also provide unending employment to poor farmers on a permanent or temporary basis (Table 8.8).

Table 8.8: Livestock Population: Cattle (2007 Census)

S. No.	District	Cattle		Total Cattle
		Crossbred	Indigenous	
1.	East Khasi H	8,789	64,485	73,274
2.	Ri-Bhoi	13,188	69,933	83,121
3.	West Khasi H	982	1,14,727	1,15,709
4.	Jaintia H	1,208	1,46,289	1,47,497
5.	East Garo H	211	1,57,823	1,58,034
6.	West Garo H	2,344	2,60,999	2,63,343
7.	South Garo H	126	46,139	46,265
	State (Overall)	26,848	8,60,395	8,87,243

Source: Animal Husbandry and Veterinary Department, Government of Meghalaya.

Poultry Development: Poultry production is one of the major components of agriculture in NER. People of this region are fond of rearing *desi* birds though the growth and production is very low, with 60-70 eggs per bird per annum and 2.5 kg. and 1.5 kg body weight per bird in males and females respectively. The per capita availability of eggs and meat in India is 34 and 700 gms. per year as against the recommendation of 180 eggs and 11 kg. meat annually for a balanced diet. The per capita availability of meat and eggs in the region is 488 gms. and 47 eggs, higher than the national requirement in eggs but lower than that required for a balanced diet. [9] However, the rural poultry production system still contributes substantially to the total egg production after meeting the household requirements. Poultry development can act as an instrument of poverty alleviation in Meghalaya. It can fulfil the nutritional requirements and help in providing subsidiary employment to farmers. The system involves less work and less expenditure and chemicals are extensively reduced which makes it environmental friendly and sustainable.

Earlier, the tribal people practiced backyard system of poultry farming. Today, it is a commercialized sector and is supporting a large network of pure line high performing layer and broiler breeding stock, and feed plants. Farm holdings with 500-1,000 birds for egg production and 100-500 birds for broiler production are now common in all the three regions of the State (Tables 8.9 and 8.10).

Table 8.9: Poultry Population (2007 Census)

S. No.	District	Fowls		Total
		Desi	Improved	
1.	East Khasi H	4,17,099	53,292	4,70,391
2.	Ri-Bhoi	3,12,519	27,422	3,39,941
3.	West Khasi H	4,57,059	37,166	4,94,225
4.	Jaintia H	3,29,824	37,479	3,67,303
5.	East Garo H	5,05,718	88,695	5,94,413
6.	West Garo H	5,65,964	25,131	5,91,095
7.	South Garo H	1,64,816	4,313	1,6,9129
	State (Overall)	27,52,999	2,73,498	30,26,497

Source: Animal Husbandry and Veterinary Department, Government of Meghalaya.

Table 8.10: Performance of Government Poultry Farms in Garo Hills [10]

Farm	Particulars of Birds Reared		Production/Supplied		
	Chicks/ Growers	Layers	Eggs Production '0000' No.	Birds Layers/Growers Sold for Breeding etc.	Broiler Reared and Sold
Rongkhon	2218	294	36.7	1372	6041
Simsangiri	920	460	79.1	425	1377
Baghmara	-	292	21.2	-	-
Phulbari	-	-	-	-	-

Source: Animal Husbandry and Veterinary Department, Government of India.

Poultry farming is a viable sector due to the following reasons:

- Requires less investment and hence provide chances to even low income groups. It involves rapid reform of profit since animal starts laying eggs at 6 months age whereas broilers are ready for meat at 6-8 weeks age.

- Food protein conversion efficiency of broilers is also exceptional at the rate of 1.9 kg. feed for 1 kg. food protein. Early marketing thus provides a year round income.
- The desi breeds require small space and can be reared easily at the backyard.
- There is no shortage of feed as most of the household garbage wastes and other agro-industrial by-products serve as poultry feed.
- It can generate full-time or part-time employment to women, children and elderly people. In case of crop failure, it stabilizes farm income when mixed farming is carried out.
- Study shows that 40 birds can supply one tonne of deep litter per year, sufficient enough to meet the full fertilizer needs of one acre of paddy or maize and half acre of crops like vegetables.

With the hardiness and disease resistant character of the tribal stock, poultry farming can turn out to be a 'rainless harvest' with egg and meat production and stock multiplication irrespective of rains or droughts.

Problems and Constraints in Livestock Management

The major challenge today in the livestock sector is how to improve the productivity and profitability of this sector. However, the farmers' decision to achieve this goal is influenced by a number of household factors and socio-economic environment. The farmer's experience and management skills, occupation, social group, land and labour endowments, access to credit, media, and deeper awareness of livestock activities are some of the factors that constrain the livestock development programme in this region if any or some of the following are not met. Some of the major constraints in livestock management are given below: [11]

- Due to the lack of livestock feed ingredients, owing to shifting cultivation and mono-cropping practiced in most parts of Meghalaya, livestock serves merely as a backyard venture rather than an economically viable enterprise. Hence, farmers find it difficult to venture into large scale production in this field.

- It has been found out that there exists a strong crop-livestock interaction. An increase in the size of holding will also increase the availability of feed and fodder. Thus, a smaller land holding will reduce the availability of feed and fodder which will in turn constrain the productivity and profitability of livestock.
- The scattered housed and hilly terrain of Meghalaya makes vaccination of common diseases extremely difficult. Lack of proper road and communication also makes it difficult to reach the people in time of crisis, which further aggravates the situation.
- The mortality rate of livestock in this region is also high due to high dependency on local and herbal treatment and medicines rather than the services provided by the animal husbandry or veterinary departments.
- Socio-economic constraints such as inadequate infrastructure, high cost of production, and low product prices also affect livestock production adversely.
- The unhygienic living conditions, contaminated feed and impure and unsafe drinking water are some of the common problems in livestock management in Meghalaya.
- Integrated slaughter houses with world class sanitary and phytosanitary conditions are absent in almost all districts of Meghalaya. Unhygienic abattoirs fall short of the standards and norms required coupled with the lack of strict vigilance and inspection, poor quality controls and absent of certification system. All these factors are major constraints to people's choice for meat and milk products in the region. Premature slaughtering of animals for meat is a national waste.
- Despite significant advances in livestock breeding, the population structure continues to be dominated by local

breeds. According to the 1992 Livestock Census, crossbred comprised only 7.5, 4.8 and 14.5 percent of cattle, sheep and pig populations respectively. Only one-third of the poultry population represents improved breeds which is even less in the State of Meghalaya.

- Studies also indicate that there is poor awareness regarding ways of improving livestock productivity to foster a sustainable livelihood—a consequence of weak public extension support for livestock.
- Many farmers did not adopt artificial insemination (AI) due to lack of confidence and awareness. Similarly, in many cases, the farmers were not aware about the benefits of vaccination and hence felt that it is not necessary.
- Though most of the urban areas are based on improved breeds and intensive input use, the rural system of production is characterized by low input and low technology. Meat production is constrained by lack of productivity augmenting technologies.

Suggestions for Improving Livestock Sector in Meghalaya

Good opportunities for growth of livestock sector in Meghalaya are evident from the rapidly rising demand for food of animal origin in Meghalaya. Steps should be taken to encourage young entrepreneurs to venture into this field and also policies should be created which will encourage farmers to improve and to increase their livestock activities as well as their economic returns so as to ensure a sustainable livelihood. Some of the important elements of livestock improvement strategy are given below:

- Providing quality services so that farmers will be motivated to adopt improved livestock farming practices, which in turn will double the productivity in terms of meat, milk, eggs and other livestock products.
- The design and the approach towards improvement of livestock sector and other related activities should be seen as self-sustainable. Hence, the required subsidy should be

provided to help farmers maintain a profitable and a sustainable business.

- Livestock farming can become an economic enterprise only if the development initiative strengthens the entire value chain. Hence, each and every component of the value chain, inbound and outbound logistics, marketing, human resource development etc. have to be taken into consideration in the entire development program.
- A good and transparent system should be established in order to supervise and to monitor the performance-linked incentives and accountability for the success of any development initiative in the State.
- The government should ensure that the established centres for livestock improvement in the State be functional and dynamic by providing the necessary skills and techniques for capacity building in order to make good profit from the industry. Similarly, efforts should be made to multiply the indigenous stocks in view of their adaptability, disease resistant nature, and better preferences by the local people.
- Better road and transport facilities; cold-storage centres; regular training of farmers; timely visit for vaccination; treatment and cure of animals; and good market are also very crucial in improving the status of livestock sector in Meghalaya which will in turn have a trickle-down effect on the livelihood of the people.

Conclusion

The situation in Meghalaya shows that the growth of livestock sector has been slower than at the national level. However, a good proportion of the landless labourers, small and marginal farmers have access to livestock resources. An increase in the growth of this sector can offer ample opportunities for household income augmentation and employment generation. Among the various agricultural enterprises, livestock production has more income generating effect on households and thus, is very effective in reducing rural income inequality. The government should ensure supportive technical, institutional and policy initiatives in order to improve the breeds, the feed availability, disease control, food safety and above all, to encourage private investments or private ventures into such an industry. Explicit focus on agro-climatic and location specific breeding, tightening the quarantine regime, stepping up research investment, conservation of animal germplasm, processing and market intelligence etc. will yield rich dividends. The above strategies have a great potential to improve the livelihood situation of the tribals of Meghalaya. A major thrust should therefore be given in this direction.

Endnotes

1. www.pib.nic.in/feature/feyr98/fe0798/PIBF2907981.html, as on May 1, 2014.
2. ICAR, Policy Brief, "Livestock Sector in India: Agenda for the Future".
3. www.en.m.wikipedia.org/wiki/Meghalaya, as on April 27, 2014.
4. Mishra, B.K. (ed.) (2012), "Livestock Production and Rural Development in India", Biotech Books, New Delhi, p. 37.
5. Ibid., p. 5.
6. Ibid., p. 39.
7. Prajapati, J.B. and Shah, B.P., (2014), "Strategies for Sustainable Growth of Indian Dairy Industry", Indian Dairy Manual, pp. 68-69.
8. Animal Husbandry and Veterinary Department, Government of Meghalaya.
9. Mishra, B.K. (ed.) (2012), "Livestock Production and Rural Development in India", Biotech Books, New Delhi, p. 259.
10. Mishra, B.K. (ed.) (2012), "Livestock Production and Rural Development in India", Biotech Books, New Delhi, p. 262.
11. Birthal, P.S., Kumar, A., Tiwari L., (eds.) (2002), Livestock in Different Farming Systems in India", Agricultural Economics Research Association, Advance Publishing Concept, New Delhi, p. viii.

References

Animal Husbandry and Veterinary Department, Government of Meghalaya.

Basic Animal Husbandry Statistics, 2012.

ICAR Policy Brief, "Livestock Sector in India: Agenda for the Future.

Mishra, B.K. (ed.) (2012), "Livestock Production and Rural Development in India", Biotech Books, New Delhi.

Sirohi, S. and Chauhan, A.K. (2014), "Current Scenario of Livestock Development and Potential Interventions for Livelihood Improvement" NDRI, Karnal.

9

Co-operative Entrepreneurship for the Endorsement of Ethno-Economy

Darshana Goswami

Introduction

Economic growth and development of any society is dependent on the basic execution of needs, resources and skills through proper asset management. The system to unify these three elements depends upon one's potential to make a structural economic process called entrepreneurship. Although this may help in growth of individual capital but for socio-economic development, the collective support of resource management is more vital which helps to make an economic equilibrium for greater interest. Here, the collective effort of strengthening socio-economic development is signified as cooperative entrepreneurship.

Though entrepreneurship is denoted as self-dependent economic growth but there is always a great part of community composition of traditional views and unique skills of a society which help in generating its own economy. Previously in rural areas, the professions were only for persistent livelihoods. Now, without changing the track and adopting modern techniques, a society can rebuild its ethno-economy. The term ethno-economy is the native economic progress of an ethnic group or society which possesses the ideas of collective entrepreneurship. Many communities and ethnic groups become economically independent and popular worldwide with unique productions like textiles, ornaments, food etc. and through which they are able to earn name, fame and financial security.

Considering the native promotion and economic track record of Lakshimpur Village of Darrang district of Assam, India, this research work would be pioneering in the study of cooperative entrepreneurship process. The study has helped to unfold several facts and consequences of unification of society under a single roof of organizational structure which has been able to direct the traditional occupation and proper wealth management. An analysis regarding the significance of collective endeavour for sustainable economic growth and development in modern context has also been carried out.

Lakshimpur tank is a historically famous tank which is locally known as *Lakshimpur Pukhuri*—tremendously a unique eco-system in the high land area of Darrang district, Assam. It was excavated along with another 359 existing tanks during the reign of the kings of *Darrangi* and *Bhuyan* dynasty during the 17th century. These tanks are rich in bio-diverse flora and fauna which plays a significant role in the socio-economic development. Our study is confined to Lakshimpur Pukhuri and its role as a cultural habitation to uplift the socio-economic scenario of the native population.

The study reveals that the population residing nearby the tank area are highly dependant on it for their livelihood and socio-economic-cultural needs and are also conscious of preserving the bio-diversity components.

Objectives of the Study

- To study the developmental activities contributing to the socio-economic life.
- To understand the key factors of sustainable development by holding the native habitation and occupation.
- To study the role of community based organizations in generating entrepreneurship and furthering the cause of peace and harmony.
- To identify the measures for a stability between human race and ecology in a global scenario.

Methodology and Database

The Lakshimpur tank was initially identified and the present size and shape was measured from the primary sources. To understand the present scenario of the tank in terms of fishery production and village lifestyle, a survey was carried out in the study area. Simultaneously, various government publications, annual reports of the concerned authorities, journals and reports from different departments viz. the District Fishery Department, District Agriculture Department and the District Forest Department of Darrang district were utilized for collecting necessary data and information.

Study Area: Lakshimpur Pukhuri is one of the oldest manmade tank of Assam known for bio-diversity conservation and sustainable development in terms of pisciculture, agro-forestry, horticulture, piggery and poultry farming etc. It is located at 91^0 55/E longitude and $26^0$30/N latitude under Kalaigaon revenue circle and is situated at a distance of 25 km. from the district headquarters in Mangaldai. It covers an area of 27.7 hectares including 13 hectares of water area with 648.8 mts. in length, 427 mts. in breadth and an average depth of 8 feet. The tank was not properly used up to 1990.

The village families living in the fringe of the swamp were totally dependent on fishery and agriculture. It was their livelihood and lifestyle. The annual income of the families was very poor and because of this, their health was also affected. In the year of 1979, the villagers united and formed the *Lakshimpur Anchalik Meen Mahal Samiti* (LAMMS) and registered it during the year 1983.

Present membership of the society is about 500 families from the farming community. It has been a successful movement which had changed and improved the socio-economic conditions of the village community through scientific fish production and utilization of other productive systems like poultry, agriculture etc. It is their own traditional habitation which has uplifted their lifestyle and economic conditions.

Lakshimpur Anchalik Meen Mahal Samiti (LAMMS)

The society of Lakhimpur Anchalik Meen Mahal Samiti has a general and an executive body. The tenure of the society is of 2 years that the general body meeting continues for 10-13 days with about 8 hours per day sitting time to transact business which is a measure of sincerity of the society. All the member families are divided into 8 units. From each unit one representative is selected to represent in the executive body. Another 8 members are co-opted. Another 7 members are drawn from general body for the posts of president, executive president, project coordinator, secretary and executive secretaries etc. Thus, the executive committee is of 23 members. Monthly sitting of the executive committee is held where secretary has to present monthly accounts and also place quarterly audit report and annual balance sheet. For further discussion here, we will follow the abbreviation LAMMS—the short form of Lakhimpur Anchalik Meen Mahal Samiti.

Objectives of LAMMS

- Proper utilization of natural and human resources.
- Increasing production and productive facilities.
- Uplifting the lifestyle.
- Building a productive communication system between villagers and the government.
- Generate employment for all.
- Women empowerment.
- Creating a market of native production.
- To stop brain-drain from villages to towns.
- To generate awareness about education, health and financial investment.

Major Activities of LAMMS

Integrated Fish Culture: It comprises multiple mode of production of fish along with friendly productive elements to fulfil the raw needs and to generate huge production in an optimum time.

Agro-pisciculture: Paddy-cum-fish culture where paddy cultivation is done near the tank. Here, the paddy gets sufficient water supply.

Piggery-Fishery: Pig-cum-fish integration where pig farms are situated near the water body and where the pig stool is used as a food supplement for the fish.

Poultry-Fishery: Duck-cum-fish integration is done where ducks get a sufficient water area.

A biological chain is compiled here to have a scientific productive system without harming the ecology.

Other Activities

Gardening: Formation of a garden of various medical plants for the fulfilment of medical requirements and preservation of rare medical herbs.

Milk Production: Increasing milk production by organizing women dairy farmers through *Lakshimpur Mahila Dugdha Udpadak Samabai Samiti Ltd.* About 50 litres of milk is sent daily to collection centres.

Public Health Protection and Environment Development Programme: It is to boost the quality of health and hygiene. LAMMS organizes public health camps, free health check up camps, seminars, workshops, awareness programmes on HIV-AIDS, phyleria, malaria, polio, relief for cancer patients etc.

Development of Roads and Communications: Construction of village roads and bridges with the help of village panchayat and government.

Tourism Development: Lakshimpur tank is the best example of bio-diversity where a large number of flora and fauna is found. Also migratory birds and rare birds like white winged wood duck, lesser whistling teel, pin-tailed duck, kingfisher, paddy bird (Ardeola gragii) are found during the winter season apart from about 1,000-1,500 different species of birds. It is a huge conservation area for Rou (*Labio Rohita*), Puthi (*Borbus Puniti*), Magur (*Clarius Assamenis*), Kaoi (*Anabas Scandens*) etc.

Besides these, every year a large number of tourists visit the place. For this purpose, LAMMS is going to generate a hub of traditional costumes and local production that will help in generating greater revenues. It is also taking steps to build guest houses for visitors, seminar hall, auditorium, playground, gymnasium and transport facilities for visit to the nearest temples and other historical places. LAAMS established rural resource development during the year 2007-08 with the help of the National Bank for Agriculture and Rural Development (NABARD), to access information and facilities, improve skills, inculcate social responsibilities among the new generation and for financial grants for schemes.

Building construction of Lakshimpur High school has been completed. Teacher salaries are borne by the LAMMS. A science centre has been established in the school campus. One agro service centre for custom hiring of tractors and power tillers for farmers has been setup. Work for setting up a local fish centre has been started for presentation of local fish genetic resources. Bank linkage of SHGs with UCO Bank, Kalaigaon and State Bank of India, Mangaldai branch has been established for starting dairy, piggery, poultry, goatery, duckery, weaving, *bari* (homestead garden) and vermicompost units. Also a model village has been established on the basis of the productive frame. LAMMS is also working for the popularization of rain water harvesting system among the villagers.

Future Plans

- To build a rural knowledge centre.
- *Magur* fish breeding.
- Hag fish culture.
- Increasing the number of nursery tanks from 12 to 30.
- Establishment of a fish feed processing mill.
- Computer training centre.
- Ambulance service.
- Medical dispensary unit.

Conclusion

LAMMS which has an annual income of approximately ₹ 13 lakh is not only a society but also a best example of the orientation of traditional knowledge and scientific system for sustainable economic development. Bio-diversity habitats can be used to generate entrepreneurship among the people. Today, social problems like communal frustrations, terrorism have arisen due to the lack of economic development. There lies a great scope to generate ethnic economy through cooperative entrepreneurship process with a worldwide production and popularity which can give economic independence and social stability. Hence, in this era of globalization, traditional occupation and wealth management should work in tandem for unification of society in order to bring peace and harmony.

References

Bordoloi, Gopal (2005) (ed), "Grassroots Institutions, Rural Development and Environment Management in North East India", Proceedings of the 6th Annual Conference of NEEA, K.B. Publications.

Das, D. (2006), "Aspects of Sustainability and Role of Institutions: A Case study of Assam", *Assam Economic Journal*, Vol. XIX.

De, U.K. (2012), "Economy of North-East India: Challenges and Tasks Ahead", Binapani Publishing House, Guwahati

Gautam, H.C. and Bezbaruah, M.P. (2006) (ed.), "Rural Transformation in North East India", Departments of Commerce and Economics, Gauhati University, Guwahati.

Kumari, Veena (2012), "Rural Development Strategies in India", Globus Press, New Delhi.

LAMMS, "Lakshimpur Anchalik Meen Mahal Samiti Annual Report, 2010-11, 2011-12, 2012-13".

Umdor, S. and B. Panda (2007), "Economic Infrastructure in North East India: An Analysis", *Man and Development*, 29(1): 113-130.

10

Women Empowerment and Self-help Groups

Swapnali Baruah

Introduction

India with 29 states and 7 Union Territories, possesses a population of 1.27 billion persons (2014), consisting of 655.8 million females and 614.4 million male population and is one of the rapidly rising economies presently. The country where land is compared or called motherland gives respect to women since times immemorial but only on the household side. It is a country with seven major rivers and numerous tributaries along with 15 mountains and is located at $28^{0}36.8'$ N and $77^{0}12.5'$ E in the northern hemisphere of the globe. *Bharatwarsha* (India) where Goddess is prayed as Durga, Laxmi, Saraswati etc. along with Gods, is a land where women are the victims of society for a long time.

Under Article 14 the longest Constitution throughout the world (i.e. India), "Right to Equality" was declared as one of the Fundamental Rights for the citizens of India. Question arises—are the women getting and enjoying equally rights with men, are they secured in real sense of the term, when the country is celebrating 69th Independence and 67th Republic Day?

Along with the rest of the world, India also celebrates 8th March and second Sunday of May as Women's Day and Mother's Day respectively. Likewise, Indian women have become modern, liberal and empowered. But are the women really empowered in India (consisting of about 3,000 castes and 25,000 sub-castes)? Can the majority of female population in the country take their own decisions liberally; can they run their business or enterprises independently?

Objectives

This paper aims at to make a brief study about the status of females in the male dominated society of North-East (NE) India. For this, the following objectives are set:

1. To study the growth of female population.
2. To study the rate of female literacy and gender gap literacy rate.
3. To study the scenario of women empowerment in the concerned NE region of India. To achieve this goal, three additional objectives are set, viz.: (a) to study the rate of female work participation in NE, (b) to study in brief about the development of SHGs in the NE region and (c) to study the participation of women in decision-making process.

Hypotheses

To fulfil the above stated objectives, following hypotheses are set:

1. Growth of NE population is negligible in comparison to the country as a whole.
2. NE India also suffers from gender gap in literacy.
3. Being the gateway of NE India, female work participation rate (FWPR) is the highest in Assam.
4. The development of NE SHGs is very good in India from financial point of view.
5. Women of NE India are more empowered in comparison to India as a whole.

Review of Literature

Numerous literature is available on women empowerment, women entrepreneurship and self-help groups (SHGs) in books, journals and internet.

The psychological sense that increases strength of individuals and communities in economic, political, social, educational, gender or spiritual ground is called empowerment. It strengthens the innate ability by way of acquiring knowledge, power and experience (Hashani et al., 1996). To Patel et al. (2013), an entrepreneur is a person who either creates new combinations of production, new products, new markets, find new sources of supply and new organizational forms…but to A. Basu, U.N. Foundation member said at the Wilson Centre (October, 2013), that empowerment is best defined as an expansion of agency throughout women's lives, not in individual sectors. It can be done through expansion of education. Rustogi (2004) opined that the use of girls in sibling care, as additional hands for helping mothers in household farm and off-farm work and so on, operates to reduce the availability of formal education for them. Does it indicate "status of women" in a society?

"Status of women" refers to the position of women in a society in relation to men. Everywhere around the globe, women are accorded a lower status than men. Women's lower status is manifested in women's low wage rates than men in all occupational fields and industries and in their limited upward mobility and unavoidable family responsibilities due to divorce, abandonment etc. in the developed countries (Mohiuddin, 1995). A rise in the share of regular wage employment could signify an improvement only if this rise is faster than the rise in the share of other two categories, viz., self-employed and casual workers (Senthuraman, 1998). Das, I. (2013), said that it requires state specific own individual policy to achieve gender development and gender equality within its borders. A detailed examination of women's status even at the district level is necessary to have the right information for effective planning and implementation of government policy.

Originated by Nobel Laureate Professor Mohammed Yunus in Bangladesh (1975), SHG movement first emerged in MYRADA (acronym of the Mysore Resettlement and Development Agency) of India in 1985. SHGs have emerged as an important strategy for empowering women and alleviate them from poverty. Poverty is one of the basic problems of the

Indian economy—one of the fastest growing economies and second most populous nation. In this country, nearly half of the human population is women and 77 percent of total rural population is female, i.e. the leading workforce. Hence, economic development to a large extent depends on women entrepreneurship, which can be promoted through women SHGs. Based on community based organizations, India's SHG movement has emerged as the world's largest and most successful network (Das et al.).

Women empowerment is supported by SHGs. Women empowerment takes place when women challenge the existing norms and culture, to effectively improve their well-being. Economic independence and ability to take decisions within the households are essential for women empowerment. SHGs have facilitated the formation of social capital, where people learn to work together for a common purpose in a group or in an organization (Putnam, 2000). SHG has had a positive impact on women members and in many cases it has been proved that SHGs promote women empowerment (Das, 2012). Serving the principle "by the women, of the women and for the women", SHG normally constitute 10-20 rural women from the same village, mostly poor, who come together to contribute two-weekly or monthly dues as savings and provide group loans to their members.

SHGs are generally facilitated by NGOs, and increasingly advise and train members in a variety of on and off farm income generating activities, i.e., entrepreneurship. Das et al. (2013) in their paper said that SHGs have emerged as an important strategy for empowering women and masses and alleviating poverty. They said that elements relating to SHGs as empowerment construct, whose mean value is positive, are considered as main elements of the empowerment construct of SHGs as perceived by direct stakeholders of SHGs. SHGs are now emerging as the predominant model for poverty eradication, women empowerment and development agencies (Panda, 2005).

Any individual woman or group of women who initiate,

organize and operate a business enterprise is called women entrepreneur (Ankurita, 2012). For Devi et al. (2014), entrepreneurship development among women can be considered a possible approach to economic empowerment of women. According to Chakrovorty, E. (2013), the scenario of growth of entrepreneurship of women in rural areas is a critical concern and if greater priority is imparted, the speedy will be the start for new enterprises in market which would propel a higher growth in the economy. Mali, D.D. said that efforts are needed for the creation of awareness of entrepreneurial opportunities among the youth, development of knowledge and skills and raising the levels of motivation for entrepreneurial career and encouragement for women entrepreneurship especially in SC/ST and OBC categories.

In his paper, Ghadoliya, M.K. said that the success of any strategy of women empowerment depends upon the level of education, hard work and social customs. Women education is sometimes also perceived as a threat by their husbands. Studying is seen as changing the identity of the partner from being subservient and domesticated (Morgen, 1995).

Question arises how to understand the economic empowerment of women? Nayak et al. (2012), in their paper made an attempt to analyze the status of women vis-à-vis men and their empowerment in terms of various socio-economic and political indicators and concluded that there is need to create awareness towards achieving the desired goal of women empowerment in the state Assam.

According to Patel et al. (2013), a majority of rural entrepreneurs are facing many problems due to non-availability of primary amenities, e.g., education, finance, technical and conceptual ability etc. making it difficult for the rural entrepreneurs to establish industries in the rural areas. It is observed that the indicators used to measure empowerment in different studies are familiar and easy to construct (Hulme et al., 2002).

To analyze the dimensions of empowerment, Luttrell et al.

(2007) identified four dimensions of empowerment, viz., economic empowerment, human and social empowerment, political empowerment and cultural empowerment.

In the current paper, an attempt has been made to make a brief analysis about the status of women in North-East (NE) India with regards to few selected socio-economic and political indicators.

Research Methodology

This paper is based on secondary data, collected from various journals, periodicals and internet. The analysis is made in terms of socio-economic and political indicators, population growth, education, employment, decision-making power and financial autonomy. Here a comparative study is made of NE India with India as a whole.

Profile of North-East India in Brief

NE India, popularly known as eight sisters, consists of Arunachal Pradesh, Assam, Manipur, Meghalaya, Mizoram, Nagaland, Sikkim and Tripura. With 2,62,185 km^2 land area and 38,857,769 persons population (2011 Census), the region covers 7.9 percent and 3.1 percent of the total land space and total population of India respectively and is located at 21.57^0 N-29.30^0 N latitude and 88^0 E-97.30^0 E longitude. With about 220 languages, the region's 90 percent borders form India's international boundaries.

Results and Discussion

Among the eight NE states, Assam seems to be the most populated state with 3.12 crore people consisting of 13.1 lakh females and 15.9 lakh male population accompanied by 17.07 percent population growth. The sex ratio seems to be the highest in Manipur (992) and the lowest in Sikkim (890), whereas at all-India level, it is 940. Assam covers 2.58 percent of India's total population and 68.6 percent of that of NER as a whole. Decadal growth of population seems to be the highest in Meghalaya at around 28 percent and negative in case of

Nagaland (-0.58) [Table 10.1]. Since NE states of India are experiencing more or less population growth, hence the first null hypothesis is rejected.

Table 10.1: Population Growth of NE India, 2011

State	Population			Population Growth	Sex Ratio
	Total	Males	Females		
(1)	(2)	(3)	(4)	(5)	(6)
Arunachal Pradesh	13,83,727	7,13,912	6,69,815	26.03	938
Assam	3,12,05,576	1,59,39,443	1,31,28,045	17.07	958
Manipur	25,70,390	12,90,171	8,57,767	12.05	992
Meghalaya	29,66,889	14,91,832	11,77,179	27.95	989
Mizoram	10,97,206	5,55,339	2,56,300	23.48	976
Nagaland	19,78,502	10,24,649	6,82,064	(-) 0.58	931
Sikkim	6,10,577	3,23,070	2,14,202	12.89	890
Tripura	36,73,917	18,74,376	13,25,291	14.84	960
India	12,101,93,422	2,32,12,792	1,81,61,195	17.64	940

Source: census2011.co.in.

Literacy is one of the important indicators to know the development in a society from economic point of view. For the purpose of census in India, a person in the age limit of seven and above, who can read with understanding in any of the language, is considered as a literate. In India, the rate of literacy has gone up from 65.38 percent (2001) to 74.04 percent (2011), showing an improvement of 9 percent. It consists of male and female literacy rate at 82.14 percent and 65.46 percent respectively (Table 10.2). Kerala is the only state occupying rank 1 throughout India in this respect (93.9 percent) for many decades, whereas Bihar occupies the last place at 63.8 percent in this regard (2011 Census). Among the NE states, the rate of literacy is the highest in Mizoram at 91.6 percent consisting of male and female literacy at 93.7 percent and 89.4 percent respectively (2011).

Arunachal Pradesh with 76 percent of literacy rate occupies the last place among the eight sisters. As per the recent information, Tripura (at 94.65 percent) has beaten Kerala (at 93.9 percent) in respect of literacy rate. As per his report on Primary Census abstract, Dr. C. Chandramouli (2013) mentioned that the gender gap in literacy rate is steadily declining and in 2011, it stood at around 16.3 points at all-India level against 21.5 points in 2001. The GLR seems to be the highest in Arunachal Pradesh and the lowest in female dominated social system in the state of Meghalaya (ranked 1). Rank of Assam in this respect was 9th at 11.5 percent in the census year 2011, whereas this rate was 16.68 percent in case of India as a whole.

So, it is said that India including NE region suffers from gender gap in literacy. Hence, the second alternative hypothesis is accepted. But at the national or regional level, it is noticed that the rate of female literacy is low than that of males. Reasons are many, viz., lack of social awareness and social customs and rituals which do not let a woman to break free.

Table 10.2: Literacy and Gender Gap in Literacy Rate in NE India, 2011

State	Rate of Literacy			GLR	Rank in GLR
	Total	Males	Females		
(1)	(2)	(3)	(4)	(5)	(6)
Arunachal Pradesh	67.0	73.7	59.6	14.1	11
Assam	73.2	78.8	67.3	11.5	09
Manipur	79.8	86.5	73.2	13.3	10
Meghalaya	75.5	77.2	73.8	3.4	01
Mizoram	91.6	93.7	89.4	4.3	03
Nagaland	80.1	83.3	76.7	6.6	04
Sikkim	82.2	87.3	76.4	10.9	-
Tripura	87.8	92.2	83.1	9.1	07
India	74.04	82.14	65.46	16.68	15

Source: Census of India (provisional) 2011; www.census2011.co.in.

With the passage of time, women have started to undertake economic activities. They are categorized as main workers (worked for 6 months or more in a reference year) and marginal workers (worked less than 6 months). As per Census 2011, 25 percent of total workers (at national level) were marginal and the remaining 75 percent were main workers. The rate stands at around 60 percent for female and 82 percent for male workers. On the other hand, about 40 percent females were engaged as marginal workers. Total working population of NE covered almost 40 percent of that of total population of the region.

Among the eight states, Assam's percentage of total working population was the highest at around 66 percent and the lowest was in Sikkim at about 2 percent. Same picture was noticed in case of percentage of male workers in Sikkim. The percentage of female workers was the highest in Arunachal Pradesh at 40 percent out of which around 75 percent were engaged as main workers. Although the percentage of female main workers was the highest in Mizoram (77 percent) but the rate of female work participation (FWPR) was only 40.3 percent. This FWPR was the highest in Manipur at 43.8 percent but the state registered around 30 percent as female marginal workers. This percentage was the highest in Tripura at about 55 percent (Table 10.3) and was the lowest in Assam (at 28.6 percent), so the third hypothesis (alternative) is rejected. Hence, it is observed that it is not necessary that the most advanced state must always be No.1 in all respects.

Table 10.3: Female Work Participation in NE India, 2011

(percentage)

State	Working Population			Female Workers		FWPR
	Total	Males	Females	Main	Marginal	
(1)	(2)	(3)	(4)	(5)	(6)	(7)
Arunachal Pradesh	3.23	59.61	40.39	74.82	24.18	40.4
Assam	65.98	47.09	18.90	48.20	51.80	28.6
Manipur	5.37	3.02	2.35	70.06	29.94	43.8
Meghalaya	6.39	3.67	2.72	60.88	39.12	42.6
Mizoram	2.68	1.60	1.08	77.42	22.58	40.3
Nagaland	6.54	3.88	2.66	69.73	30.27	28.9
Sikkim	1.70	1.07	0.63	69.73	30.27	28.9
Tripura	8.10	5.76	2.34	44.59	55.41	30.9

Calculations from NSSO (2011).
Source: www.census2011.co.in.

SHGs have helped women to gain economic and social empowerment. NER of India is not exceptional in this regard. However, the banking sector has faced problems to support SHGs financially. In order to achieve the mission of reaching those families who do not have access to credit by any formal financial institution, the National Bank for Agriculture and Rural Development (NABARD) introduced the "SHG-Bank Linkage Programme" as a pilot project in 1992. Later it was extended to all commercial banks (CBs), regional rural banks (RRBs) and co-operative banks. By March 2002, the Programme covered 7.8 million families with 90 percent women workers.

Thus, SHGs have been linked to CBs, RRBs and co-operative banks. ₹ 79,675.59 lakh of loans was extended to the NER of India as micro credit through SHG-Bank Linkage as on March 31, 2013. But savings of SHGs in the NE region during the same period was estimated at ₹ 13,010.63 lakh only (Table 10.4). From the analysis of Table 10.4 and 10.5, it is observed that among the N-E states, Assam occupied rank 1 regarding the number of SHGs but a gloomy picture is evident regarding the amount of savings of these SHGs with the financial institutions. So, the fourth hypothesis is rejected. Thus, the SHGs must set their goals as to promote savings and credit activities to promote empowerment of women (Choudhury et al., 2009).

A woman is said to be empowered when she takes or participates in household decisions, can go to needy places, possesses financial freedom etc. These three points have been considered in Table 10.6. As per the Table, at all-India level, around 37 percent women participated in family or household decisions and can go to markets, health facilities and outside the community whereas only 17 percent females operated bank accounts. This rate was the highest in Sikkim at 21 percent and the lowest in Nagaland at 7 percent. In Mizoram, 75 percent women possessed liberty to move to needy places whereas in female-oriented social system of Meghalaya, 77 percent women took family decisions. Thus, it is not wrong to think that the status of women is comparatively better in the tribal societies (Handsdal, 2012; Burman, 2012).

Table 10.4: Savings of SHGs with Banks, March 31, 2013

(in ₹ lakh)

State	Commercial Banks		Regional Rural Banks	
	No. of SHGs	Savings Amount	No. of SHGs	Savings Amount
(1)	(2)	(3)	(4)	(5)
Assam	87,203	7,037.21	1,59,147	3,458.00
Arunachal Pradesh	3,074	155.44	1,538	227.68
Manipur	4,929	102.55	6,106	110.30
Meghalaya	3,264	228.21	3,550	245.47
Mizoram	1,128	46.56	1,336	547.12
Nagaland	3,219	147.36	746	13.23
Sikkim	3,529	79.48	-	-
Tripura	10,438	219.34	-	-
NER	1,16,784	8,016.15	1,72,423	4,601.80
India	40,76,986	5,53,257.05	20,38,008	1,52,710.20

Contd...

States	Cooperative Banks		Total	
	No. of SHGs	Savings Amount	No. of SHGs	Savings Amount
(1)	(6)	(7)	(8)	(9)
Assam	24,722	255.55	2,71,072	10,750.76
Arunachal Pradesh	421	28.97	5,033	412.09
Manipur	1,621	22.39	12,656	235.24
Meghalaya	2,759	41.98	9,573	515.66
Mizoram	653	18.53	3,117	612.21
Nagaland	4,513	25.26	8,478	185.85
Sikkim	-	-	3,529	79.48
Tripura	-	-	10,438	219.34
NER	34,689	392.68	3,23,896	13,010.63
India	12,02,557	1,15,758.22	73,17,551	8,21,725.47

Source: *Status of Microfinance in India, 2012-13*, NABARD.

Although the above discussion gives a bright picture of shining NE India (to some extent) but at the same time in this region, time to time women get harassed from many sides. Data shows that cases relating to attempt to murder in Assam during the year 2012 were 670, rape was 1,716 and dowry deaths were 5,077. The number of cases related to crimes against women and girls are on the rise. The number of rape cases increased from 1,631 (2009) to 1,721 (2010) in India.

During the same period, molestation cases increased from 1,389 to 1,611 and the number of reported trafficking cases also increased from 41 to 47. The increase in the total number of cases related to cruelty by husband rose from 4,355 to 5,189 during 2009-10, attesting a high incidence of domestic violence.

Table 10.5: Bank Loans Outstanding Against SHGs, March 31, 2013

(in ₹ lakh)

State	Commercial Banks		Regional Rural Banks	
	No. of SHGs	Loan O/S Amount	No. of SHGs	Loan O/S Amount
(1)	(2)	(3)	(4)	(5)
Assam	61,391	33,809.113	52,385	27,289.18
Arunachal Pradesh	238	224.11	75	80.75
Manipur	3,015	1,683.12	1,576	409.45
Meghalaya	1,277	604.17	862	836.58
Mizoram	69	77.07	2,568	1,808.49
Nagaland	1,919	1,341.09	66	147.46
Sikkim	2,856	1,237.84	-	-
Tripura	6,860	5,598.95	-	-
NER	77,625	44,575.48	57,532	30,571.91
India	26,43,971	26,63,944.38	13,27,367	10,52,122.91

Contd...

State	Cooperative Banks		Total	
	No. of SHGs	Loan O/S Amount	No. of SHGs	Loan O/S per SHG
(1)	(6)	(7)	(8)	(9)
Assam	7,714	3,758.11	1,21,490	64,856.42
Arunachal	79	82.92	392	387.78
Manipur	-	-	4,591	2,092.57
Meghalaya	237	320.83	2,376	1,761.58
Mizoram	30	61.04	2,667	1,946.60
Nagaland	443	305.30	2,428	1,793.85
Sikkim	-	-	2,856	1,237.84
Tripura	-	-	6,860	5,599.00
NER	8,503	4,528.20	1,43,660	79,675.59
India	4,80,096	2,21,462.43	44,51,434	39,37,529.72

Source: *Status of Microfinance in India, 2012-13,* NABARD.

Table 10.6: Women Participation in Decision-making/ Women Empowerment

(percent)

States	Currently married women who usually participate in household decisions	Women of age 15-49 who are allowed to go alone to three places (market, health facility and outside the community)	A bank or saving account that women themselves use
(1)	(2)	(3)	(4)
Arunachal Pradesh	53.5	40.2	19
Assam	60.9	35.3	11.7
Manipur	69.4	53.5	8
Meghalaya	77.3	28.1	16.9
Mizoram	70.4	75.4	8.1
Nagaland	73.1	25.4	7.4
Sikkim	58.7	50.9	20.9
Tripura	30.2	36.8	18.7
India	36.7	36.8	16.2

Sources: NFHS-3; Kishore and Gupta, 2009.

According to National Crime Record Bureau's report, the highest number of violent crimes were reported from Assam (54.2 percent) followed by Manipur (44.6 percent), Kerala (92.7 percent) and Delhi (34.7 percent). The all-India average was 22.7 percent.

According to published sources, the numerical figure regards women harassment in Assam stood at 17,449 in the year 2013 listing the state at 7th throughout India in the list of women harassment cases. It indicates that at average daily 48 such cases are happening in the state. On an average during the year 2013, 1,937 rape cases happened in the state, against 33,707 rape cases in India.

Daily this rate translates to 93 in the state (average). Cases of Bornali Deb (2005, Assam), Laxmi (2007, Assam), G.S. Road, Guwahati (2012, Assam), Damini (2012, Delhi), Shakti Mills (2013, Mumbai), Dr. Sarita (2014, Dibrugarh, Assam), Meghalaya (June, 2014) etc. bear the burning proof of women status in India, mainly in NE India.

Suggestions

What government is doing is good. But we are to make them "better than the best". Females have to think for themselves not in a selfish way but for their development so that they can enjoy the Fundamental Right of "Right to Equality" truly. Suggestions in this regard are as follows.

For women empowerment, entrepreneurship has to develop. For it, good entrepreneurs have to be generated which can be done through education, development of skills, provision of vocational training and alleviation of poverty. All these are accompanied by other factors also. In fact, development of social overhead capital and control of population is the best solution to the problem. Hence, development of women entrepreneurship through SHGs can be a good step in empowering women in NE India.

Conclusion

Even now, mass medias headlines are captured mostly by such news that proves again and again the insecurity of females in Assam (e.g., minor girl gang raped, brother attacked, pregnant lady got raped in ambulance, girl child of 6 years old kidnapped from night bed and raped etc.).

Some private regional news channels (popular at the national and international level) telecast such news again and again that many a time it becomes irritating and a headache to switch on such channels. Motive of such media might be positive but at the same time it provokes many to follow such wrong path.

Male oriented Indian society anyhow tries to keep women always below them. At the same time, our present Prime Minister, Shri Narendra Modi during his 1st address to the nation while celebrating 68th Independence Day of India, said "our heads hang in shame", speaking against the backdrop of rising rape cases.

He asked every parent to keep a tab on their sons and hold them accountable much like the way they put restrictions on their sons as they put on their daughters. However, in this 21st century and if we have to go ahead, the saying of Emily Dickinson would be worth mentioning,

"We never know how high we are
Till we are called to rise
And then, if we are true to plan
Our statures touch the skies".

References

Burman and Roy, J.J. (2012), "Status of Tribal Women in India", *Mainstream*, Vol. 1(2).

Chakravorty, E. (2013), "The Rural Women Entrepreneurial Edge", *IOSR Journal of Humanities and Social Sciences,* Vol. 10(1).

Choudhury, J. and Devi, R. (2009), "Women's Participation in Economic Development: Role of SHGs", in Konwar, K. and Das, S. (eds.), Role of Women in Socio-economic Upliftment of Assam, Purbanchal Prakash, Guwahati.

Das, K. and Bhowal, A. (2013), "Self-help Groups as an Empowerment Model: Perceptions of Direct Stakeholders", *American Journal of Rural Development.*

Das, S.K. (2012), "Best Practices of Self-help Groups and Women Empowerment: A Case of Barak Valley of Assam", *Far East Journal of Psychology and Business,* Vol. 7(2).

Devi, A. and Goswami, G. (2014), "Women Entrepreneurship Development in Assam with Special Reference to Kamrup District, India", *The Clarion Multidisciplinary International Journal,* Vol. 3(1).

Fernandez, A.P. (2007), "History and Spread of the Self-help Affinity Group Movement in India".

Hansdak, E.M. (2012), "The Status of Women" in Fr. Agapit Turkey (ed.), Responding to India's Social Challenges: Promoting Tribal Rights and Culture.

Hulme, D. and Mosley, P. (1996), "Finance against Poverty", *Journal of Micro Finance,* Vol. 1(109).

Kishore, S. and Gupta, K. (2009), "A Report on Gender Equality and Women's Empowerment on the Basis of National Family Health Survey (NFHS)-3", Mumbai.

Mohiuddin, Y. (1995), "Country Ranking of Women's Status: An Alternative Index".

Morgan, A. (1995), "Adult Change and Development: Learning and Peoples' Lives", in D. Dewart (ed.), One World Many Voices: Quality in Open and Distance Learning.

Narang, U. (2012), "Impact of Self-help Groups-Bank Linkage Programme in India", *International Journal of Trade and Commerce–IIARTC,* Vol. 1(2): 220-228.

Nayak, P. and Mahanta, B. (2012), "Women Empowerment in Assam", Social Science Research Network.

Panda, R.K. (2005), "Emerging Issues of Rural Credit", APH Publishing Corporation, New Delhi.

Putnam, R. (2000), "Bowling Alone: The Collapse and Revival of American Community", Simon & Schuster, New York.

Rustogi, P. (2004), "Significance of Gender-related Development Indicators: An Analysis of Indian States", *Indian Journal of Gender Studies,* Vol. 11(3).

Seibel, H.D. and Dave, H.R. (2002), "Commercial Aspects of Self-help Group Banking in India: A Study of Bank Transaction Costs", NABARD, Mumbai.

Websites

www.aijsh.org
www.census2011.gov.org
www.col.org
www.ibnlive.com
www.indiaonlinepages.com
www.indiatvnews.com
www.ifad.org
www.ijarcsms.com
www.myrada.org
www.nedan.in
www.newsecuritybeat.org
www.papers.ssrn.com
www.pubssciepub.com
www.poseidon01.ssrn.com
www.sgsrjournals.com
www.seea.org.in
www.shodhganga.inflibnet.ac.in
www.telegraphindia.com

www.w.sa-dhan.net
www.worldpulse.com

11

Entrepreneurial Skill Development for Self-employment

Arambam Jolly Devi and Arambam Geetanjali

Introduction

Training and skill upgradation has been one of the key concerns of the Government since the days of foundation of our planning, addressing to the issue of economic development (Pathak and Tomar, 2012). The 12th Plan (2012-2017) document mentions that skill development is critical for achieving faster, sustainable and inclusive growth on the one hand and for providing decent employment opportunities to the growing young population on the other. Countries with higher and better levels of knowledge and skills respond more effectively and promptly to challenges and opportunities of globalization.

Unemployment and poverty continues to plague the Indian economy despite almost half a century of planned development—the magnitude as well as the percentage of unemployment and underemployment has been on the rise.

The unemployment situation in India, especially in the North-Eastern Region, has become a problem that deserves immediate attention. India's problem today may not exactly be a shortage of jobs. It may be shortage of employable skills. India's growing economy requires a large and skilled workforce. However, the lack of quality trainers and training institutes has created roadblocks to growth. Skill shortage is evident in every sector of the economy. Absence of reliable information on the actual growth in employment by specific occupational categories makes it difficult to determine either the number of jobs being created in each field or the unsatisfied demand for various types of skills. Besides this, there is a huge mismatch between demand and supply of skilled workforce.

Moreover, generating employment opportunities have become all the more challenging with the change in the technology and changes noticed in the manufacturing and services sector. Development of trade related specific skills and management skills have become crucial to be in the competition.

Developing the spirit of entrepreneurship among the youth in the present day context is considered to be very important in the region, because government cannot provide jobs for all kinds of unemployed youths. By providing entrepreneurial skills, they will create their own employment and self-employment opportunity which is the need of the hour. During the working lives, people must be given the chance to maintain and enhance their employability through lifelong learning, thus ensuring that the economy is provided with a sufficiently skilled workforce. We are today living in a dynamic world and an organization cannot prosper and progress unless it has the capacity to manage change. It is the youth who should be targeted to make the change and manage the change. Youth are the main pillars of our future generation; they need to be motivated not only as job seekers but also as job creators.

Skills linked to production planning, costing, quality control, design and technology development, marketing among others, need focused attention to enable producers to compete in the open market (Patel, 2013). A systematic planning, acquiring necessary entrepreneurial knowledge and positive mindsets are the basic requirements for the youth to be self-employed.

North-Eastern Region

The North-Eastern Region is industrially one of the most backward regions of the country and inadequacy of local human resources is one of the major causes of industrial backwardness. In this region, there has always been a shortage of trained personnel in various functional areas of management.

North-Eastern areas are untouched by the development programs of the Government. The officials and policy makers, who prepare plans and programs, should adhere to the ground reality of the problems of North-Eastern States and to identify the factors that hinder the developmental process.

Comprising of eight states of Assam, Arunachal Pradesh, Manipur, Meghalaya, Mizoram, Nagaland, Sikkim and Tripura, North-East India represents a distinct geographical entity with its diverse resources and geo-climatic conditions. The region has a population of 3,84,93,000 persons as per the estimates of Census of 2001,which is 3.75 percent of the total population of the country as a whole. It is estimated that at present there are nearly 27 lakh registered and unregistered unemployed youths in the region (Kalita, 2006). Table 11.1 shows the comparison of characteristics of North-East unemployed persons (youths) with other parts of the country.

The region also perhaps continued to remain low in ranking in nurturing regional common interests and sentiments. The leaders of the region who could have positioned themselves in the mainstream politics, largely failed to raise the issue of regional interests in the national forum aggressively and effectively. Instead, they approached the Centre with begging bowl, replicating an inferior image of the region as a whole. On the other hand, the Central power provided substantive funds to the region without any strategic plan. In doing so, they perhaps, were mostly overwhelmed by the principle "we should judge results not by statistics or by the amount of money spent but by the quality of human character that has evolved (Deb, 2011).

There are lots of lacunas regarding the skill development programs in the region starting from the wrong selection of the beneficiaries/trainees. Now, the true motto lies in upgrading the skills of people for socio-economic development in the

North-Eastern region substantially with full commitment from the trainers as well as the trainee side. It is a big challenge to each one of us to see where we stand economically and socially in the country. It is important to encourage men and women to take up entrepreneurship as a career for the growth and development of the region.

Table 11.1: Comparison of Characteristics of North-East Unemployed Persons with Other Parts of the Country

S. No.	Unemployed Youths of Other Parts of the Country	Unemployed Youths of North-East Region
1.	Desire to become self-employed	Desire to become self-employed is in the dormant state
2.	Preference for government job is limited	Preference given to white collared and secured jobs
3.	A congenial environment exists which is supportive towards being self-employed	No congenial environment exists which can motivate the youth
4.	Ready and willing to do hard work	Easy earning attitude
5.	Majority of the unemployed are aware about self-employment schemes and come forward to take up	Unemployed are not aware of the opportunities of self-employment schemes
6.	Up to date information available which is acquired by the youth	Very difficult to get proper information
7.	Active support system and advice are available	Support system and advice are available but not satisfactory
8.	Interested to involve in modern types of activities	Due to lack of proper knowledge and awareness, people generally prefer traditional activities
9.	Ready to move everywhere for employment	Majority of the unemployed are not ready to go outside their native place

Source: Kalita, J.C. (2006), "Self-employment through Entrepreneurship", pp. 16-17.

Skill Development

Skill development has been the major focus of the central government to increase the employment opportunities among the youth and also to cater to the demand of skilled labour force in the industry (Gautam and Bhardwaj, 2013). Besides, it is a common knowledge that our education system, even the much trumpeted New Education Policy, has failed in its primary aim of meeting aspirations of individuals, requirements of society needs and challenges of a growing economy. The basic reason behind this failure is inability to equip our youths for gainful employment or role after completion of long and costly courses of study. This calls for a link between entrepreneurial development and education. To this end, we shall have to restructure the educational courses so that our students get transformed into successful entrepreneurs. We should prepare our students to enable them for the innovative ideas, new ventures and latest techniques to match the international challenges in the context of new demands. It has to keep in mind the vision of India becoming the fourth largest economy in the world by 2020 and for this pace of growth it has to promote skills and technologies which will be required of Indians by that time (Watni, 2012).

A skill may be defined as the learned ability to carry out a task with pre-determined results often within a given amount of time, energy, or both. In other words, the abilities that one possesses—education, training, employment, enterprise and work are wide-ranging multifaceted concepts which relates to skill for livelihood promotion. Entrepreneurial education and training programs can intervene as basic literacy programs to earn livelihoods. 'A livelihood comprises the capabilities, assets (including both material and social resources) and activities required to earn one's living. A livelihood is sustainable when it can cope with and recover from stresses and shocks and maintain or enhance its capabilities and assets both now and in the future, without undermining the natural resource base' (Chaturvedi, 2007). Skill upgradation will enable many more people to be trained and improve their prospects of employment by placing greater emphasis on equipping them with skills that are currently required. The main objective of such program is to secure an adequate supply of people with up-to-date skills to meet the demands of new technologies upon which economic growth must be based

(Kumar, 2001).

The Twelfth Five Year Plan (2012-17) also focuses on mainstreaming skill formation in the formal education system right from class 10 onwards. The Third Session of Standing Labour Committee organized by Ministry of Labour and Employment, Government of India in February, 2009, focused on skill deficit mapping. The National Skill Development Agency (NSDA) which would be the single point focus for all skill development activities will take all possible steps to meet skilling targets as envisaged in the 12th Five Year Plan and beyond.

A National Policy on Skill Development was also formulated in 2009 with the aim to provide skills to 500 million people by 2022. The policy emphasizes on dynamic, demand-based skill initiatives which are aligned with government policies on economy and development. The 12th Plan has also set a target of creation of 50 million work opportunities in the non-farm sector and creating an equivalent pool of skilled manpower by the end of the plan (Sanghi and Sensarma, 2013). To meet these targets, skill development is a must, especially for the youths who are the main assets of a country in future. The skill development/upgradation programs should be very effective and efficient.

The Government of India is implementing several schemes on skill development with the objective of enhancing employability through skilling up of the skilled, and re-skilling of existing and new entrants to the labour force (Table 11.2).

The aforesaid programs are being implemented for the overall economic development of a country in general and skill development in particular.

Skill development or upgradation requires lot of inputs where feasibility of the potential prospect, needs to be analyzed in depth. First, for whom (beneficiaries/trainees) the skill is required and what type (trade). Whether, the skill he/she is going to learn will benefit (self-employment) in future or not. If so, to what extent and what are the market avenues. These are some of the issues which need concerns in time.

Table 11.2: Major Programs for Skill Development in India

S. No.	Program	Objectives and Targets
1.	Craftsmen Training Scheme (CTS)	Systematic training to school leavers
2.	Skill Department Initiative on Modular Employable Skills (MES)	Vocational training to school leavers, existing workers, ITI graduates etc.
3.	National Rural Livelihood Mission (NRLM)/Aajeevika Skill	Provides placement linked market driven skill trainings to rural BPL youth
4.	Rural Self Employment Training Institutes (RSETIs)	Free unique intensive short-term residential self employment training to rural youth
5.	National Urban Livelihood Mission (NULM)	Skill formation/upgradation to undertake self-employment
6.	Support to Training and Employment Program (STEP)	Upgradation of skills,marketing, credit linkages and sustainable employment for women
7.	*Parvaaz*	Education, skills and employment for minority school drop outs
8.	Entrepreneurial Skill Development Program (ESDP)	Upgrade skills of prospective entrepreneurs, existing and new workers for SC/ST/OBC/women
9.	*Hunar Se Rozgar* Scheme	Free skills in hospitality sector for youth
10.	Polytechnics	Skills after class X, 3 Years conventional programme
11.	The Integrated Skill Development Scheme (ISDS)	Textiles related skill to women, SC/ST, handicapped, BPL
12.	MSME Tool Room	Technical upgradation,vocational training to school dropouts
13.	Credit for Vocational Courses	Loan amount of ₹ 20,000 to ₹ 1.50 lakh for underprivileged and weaker section youths
14.	National Skills Qualification Framework (NSQF)	Progression and participation through vertical and horizontal mobility
15.	Labour Market Information System	Quantitative and qualitative information and intelligence on labour market

Source: Compiled from various sources.

North-Eastern States being an isolated region and with

land locked areas and poor connectivity makes the people more helpless. Though the Central Government gives a lot of emphasis for developing the under-developed states, still there exist vast gaps starting from the lack of proper and accurate information in time.

Self-employment

According to National Sample Survey Organization, self-employment means one who employs himself. Some other economists say that one who performs his activities without other helps is said to be self-employed (Kalita, 2006). Self-employment can indicate the one who involves himself in his activities with a motto to earn and at the same time create employment opportunities for others.

Employability is understood to be the acquisition of sound knowledge in a specialized field, along with skills and competence which enables an individual to exercise the occupation he or she has learnt immediately after completing training (Madhukar, 2003).

Employment holds a pivotal position in an individual's life. There is no limitation in learning a new thing for becoming self-employed. Learning is a process and there is no such trade which is considered not important. If one excels in a particular trade there is always a way forward. It just needs a positive attitude, knowledge and skill.

To achieve all round development of the region, we have to improve backwardness of the people by utilizing the resources including potential human resource to create self-employment. Education and employment policies in India, if go together, will surely increase the skilled labour force.

Some Related Issues

1. Emphasis has been on general education, with skill upgradation training at the receiving end.
2. Simply leaving a participant with a certificate to fend for himself/herself has added to the plethora of

unemployment.

3. Low level of follow up measures to see what the participants in a training program have achieved and whether there has been a progress in terms of employability and income generation.
4. Lack of capital leaves them with little option to choose from plants, tools and technologies.
5. The other business houses which have come in the region are basically setting up franchise units such as in mobile phones, internet connection courses etc.
6. The youth who are employed in unorganized sector look unsettled and are trying constantly to search for better opportunities outside the region.
7. Increasing modernization and the technological wave have made indigenous methods of weaving, textiles, traditional medicines etc. on the verge of becoming extinct.
8. Lack of intermediate goods, especially in trade where packaging is a must.
9. Transportation costs for raw materials as well as finished products are high, which raises the cost and reduces profit margin.

Suggestive Measures

1. Skill upgradation and training programs can intervene as basic literacy programs to earn livelihoods.
2. Forward and backward linkages should be developed from procurement to marketing.
3. Strong monitoring and evaluation systems with collaborative programs should be encouraged so that placement opportunities, exposures and field experiences are enhanced.
4. Flexibility to suit the needs and aspirations of different categories of learners.
5. Schemes and subsidy programs should be advertised at the grassroots level and those who are availing, need to be monitored regularly by the concerned authorities.

6. Training should be based on the local resources (value addition) which are easily accessible.
7. Institutes for training and education could well be a benchmark for revival (indigenous knowledge) and survival (linking such knowledge with trades) as well as for looking into contemporary realities, keeping in mind the training factor.
8. The products should be of standard and marketable. Virtual market should be upgraded.
9. Infrastructure facilities should be created with the participation of the private sector.

Conclusion

Globalization and the revolution in information and communication technology have signalled the need for a new human-cantered development paradigm. Skill upgradation for becoming self-employed as an integral component of lifelong learning has a crucial role to play in this new era of development. Every profession demands certain specific skills and competence on the part of its practitioners. Skill development or upgradation should be planned in such a way that it serves all the purposes keeping in mind the demand and supply gap. One should demonstrate certain skills and competencies which can influence learning in the students and help them achieve their goals of life.

References

Chaturvedi, Ramesh (2007), "Educational and Vocational Guidance and Counselling", Cresent Publishing Corporation, New Delhi, p. 133.

Deb, Sukamal (2011), "Problems and Prospects of Entrepreneurship in North East India", in Entrepreneurship and Rural Development in North East India, Ram Krishna Mandal (ed.), DVS Publishers Guwahati, p. 122.

Gautam, Harendra Raj and Bhardwaj, M.L. (2013), "New Arenas in Rural Employment", *Kurukshetra*, Vol. 61, No. 4, February, pp. 8-11.

Kalita, J.C. (2006), "Unemployment Problem and Entrepreneurship:

Self Employment through Entrepreneurship", Indian Institute of Entrepreneurship, Guwahati, pp. 15-17.

Nath, H.D. Dwaraka (2013), "Strategies for Employment Generation in Rural India: A Critical Evaluation", *Kurukshetra*, Vol. 61, No. 4, February, pp. 27-31.

Patel, Mahendra (2013), "Rural Industries: Harnessing Potential to Generate Employment", *Kurukshetra*, Vol. 61, No. 4, February, pp. 45-48.

Pathak, K.N. and Tomar, J.S. (2012), "Skill-Upgradation in Five Year Plans", *Yojana*, August, pp. 69-72.

Sanghi, Sunita and Sensarma, Kuntal (2013), "Skills for All", *Yojana*, September, pp. 57-61.

Sharma, Arpita (2014), "Rural Development Schemes through Years", *Kurukshetra*, Vol. 62, No. 4, February, pp. 12-15.

12

Entrepreneurship and Promotion of Tourism

Bindusar Irom

Introduction

With the birth of globalization, the concept of entrepreneurship has been well accepted by the less developed and developing countries. Manipur is projected as a promising destination rich in tourism resources in the form of serene natural beauty, favourable climate throughout the year, fascinating range of flora and fauna, co-existence of several communities in harmony, indigenous sports, lifestyles, arts and culture, fairs and festivals, rich heritage, handlooms and handicrafts, exotic cuisines, etc. Manipur is known for its unexploited natural availability of abundant human resources which are the basic factors of economic development. On the contrary, the indigenous people/locals lack tourism awareness. Also, no efforts have been made by the government to make the indigenous people utilize the benefits of tourism. The improper maintenance and functioning of places of tourist interest and hotels could be thought of as examples of failure on the part of the government. The paper attempts to find a feasible solution for making entrepreneurship as one its vital ingredients in developing tourism in Manipur.

Need for Entrepreneurship Development

The entrepreneurs contribute to society by nurturing creativity, new products, and especially new ideas into the existing platform. There is growing evidence that entrepreneurs play a vital role in business and economic growth. For example, the coming up of The Classic Hotel, under the leadership of Dr. Th. Dhabali Singh, making it the only three star classified hotel in the state is unquestionably an illustration that the entrepreneurial investment can also give back huge returns. It is also a known fact that not only the service industry but the hotel will also prove to be a boon for development of the service providers and subsidiary suppliers. His efforts of bringing up a lucrative hotel in the heart of a city mired with conflicts are laudable.

Further, the project of "Classic Grande" under the same leadership targeted for five star classifications will also expedite the level of standards and state of the art facilities. With these two units, the revenue will be generated for the state government in the form of taxes; administrative fees and the employment of almost 500 staff, who will be able to earn their livelihood. Entrepreneurship also yields more satisfying employment opportunities to people who have had bad job experience before, and thereby increasing stability and consequently the economic prosperity.

The need for entrepreneurship in the State can be determined in a way that it helps in generating income and employment, which in turn will help solve insurgency problem in the state to some extent. The serious matter of unemployment cannot be solely solved by creating more jobs in the public sector and other various government departments; there must be development of micro, small and medium entrepreneurship for self-employment and expansion of job opportunities.

For this, the educated youth of the region must be trained and involved in entrepreneurship oriented vocations for promoting locality based tourism. In a nutshell, it is emphasized through this paper that the development of Manipur depends to an extent on the entrepreneurial activities and that depends primarily on active participation of the local entrepreneurs in promoting their local specialties.

Challenges of Entrepreneurship Development

For a state like Manipur, the major factor hampering

entrepreneurship development is the prevailing law and order situation. For local entrepreneurs, it is also difficult to pool capital for new ventures with the kind of risk involved. Further, it becomes even more complicated to avail loans from financial institutions and banks unless these young entrepreneurs have high profiles or have current existing family businesses to give collateral to banks. Another factor is the absence of consistent marketing and mediocre quality of the products which restricts the inflow of tourists to the state. Another major hindrance is the *bandh*/blockade called by various organizations along the highways despite it being declared as unconstitutional and illegal by the Supreme Court in 1997; the State continues to suffer from this epidemic affecting trade and commerce directly. Daily wage earners and business establishments also bear the brunt affecting the development of the region in the long run.

Development of Hospitality Service Industry

The success of the hotel industry is definitely tied up with tourism. There exists a serious lack of service industry, hotel services and allied facilities. Currently, the demand for hotels is mostly confined to business associates, medical representatives, NGOs, etc. thus rendering it difficult for this sector to thrive. The visits of foreign tourists are also confined to specific events such as their visit during the Sangai festival in the month of November, tourists from Japan to see the war memorial at Maibam Lokpa Ching, British nationals visiting the war cemetery etc. However, such visits depend on the specific interests of the visitors; it could be said that none had come to see Manipur from the idea of the place being a tourist destination.

A major contribution of hotel income comes from outdoor catering of social functions. The coming in of domestic clients to explore Manipur does not happen often. This illustrates the absence of a robust tourism industry. There is no doubt that the state does not lack on enormous variety of tourist spots and its potential. The question is how to convert these tourist spots into attractive destinations so that the general mindset of the outsiders and the locals turn towards a more positive perception. To market hotels, it also becomes necessary to improve the allied facilities and services so that the customers feel homely during their stay. Entrepreneurship can take its shape in promoting and marketing the existing tourism potential in conformity with its characteristics.

Prospects

Manipur is experiencing development in the field of tourism with the aim to bring a massive change in overall socio-economic condition of the State by exploiting the immense tourism potential of the State by cultivating the benefits of tourism development. One could foresee a positive change in the sector following the conversion of Tulihal, Imphal Airport to an international one and more so with the opening of eastern frontier with the Southeast Asian countries. It is believed that the numerous projects and schemes initiated by the government will add to the value. Moreover, growing involvement of organized private sector in recent times has managed to tap the industry in a successful way. Despite failing in cultivating tourism, the demand for room accommodation is still on the rise. It may be due to the fact that the trade and commerce is increasing and market for the same is expanding. In addition, the guests who arrive at the hotels often request to visit Moreh-Tamu on a leisure tour.

Manipur also does not lack in human resources and has qualified personnel from various prestigious hotel institutes like IHM, enabling their expertise in the field of hotel management. The Ministry of Tourism certified program "Hunar Se Rozgar Tak" has been implemented, enabling unskilled locals to get trained and impart them knowledge of the hotel industry. With such certification, they can apply for jobs in the hotel industry via the skills gained. The state mechanism of removing PAP (Protected Area Permit) is also a positive signal in promotion of tourism. With the introduction of PPP (public private partnership) model attracting the private parties to take the management of government undertakings on lease, would also yield a positive result. An example can be cited referring to Hotel Imphal and Sendra Resorts which has been under trial and has been handed over to the same entity, "The Classic Hotel".

Massive changes have thereafter been brought in the structure as well as the standards, benchmarking itself to a three star category hotel and it may also be noted that this hotel which has been incurring a minimal profit has finally been able to see an increase in profit margin due to its functioning.

Challenges of Hotels and Resorts

Coming up with high standard hotels and resorts has not been an easy task as such hotels require certain levels of machines and equipments which are not easily available in the local market. Such items are procured from different cities and due to *bandh* and blockades along the National Highway, the items do not arrive on schedule, hampering the smooth operations. Thus, such blockades called due to demands of various organizations have also been a major constraint. Such blockades do not have a time span leading to increase in the costs of daily consumables, essential commodities and fuel etc. The government has for the longest time not taken any immediate action to resolve the existing issues. Further complicating the difficulties, is the various armed outfits that often have their own demands, monetary or otherwise. The prevailing law and order situation does not support in promoting tourism. There is a pre notion that Manipur is a conflict ridden state and this has become the biggest factor for tourists avoiding the state.

It can also be added that it is not just the tourists but also the local populace which does not visit tourist spots like Keibul Lamjao National Park, Shirui hills etc. out of fear. It becomes an utmost necessity to first encourage the locals to visit such places without fear. Safety of the tourists is also one of the major issues and who is liable for the same should be ascertained. For instance, the existence of Assam Rifles regiment alongside Sendra resorts and Manipur rifles at the Kangla Fort is an example of military occupation of the tourist spots. Laws like AFSPA (Armed Forces Special Powers Act, 1958) have also drastically affected the tourism potential of the state making it one of the most hostile places in India. Poor provision of infrastructure viz. roads, electricity, transport, etc. has also affected tourism. It is ironic that poor infrastructure rather than the governance issue gets relegated as not an issue of the government, as many other issues nag the state. A host of other such issues gets labelled due to the problem of insurgency. As tourism industry is in a bad shape, it becomes very difficult to promote or market the hotels from tourism perspective.

Implications of New Ideas

Generation of innovative ideas and exploring the untapped potential of tourism is the top most priority. It is seen that numerous eco-parks or gardens initiated by local entrepreneurs have come up recently in various parts of the state. It is also vital that not just the implementation of new projects but also to maintain the same decorum throughout its operation is vital. Local entrepreneurs can also come up with various innovative plans like village tourism, home stay, camp tourism etc. which is still unexplored. The idea behind this is that it is not seasonal, requires low investment and the locals can promote their specialty in a highly creative manner. Such product profile will benefit the locals in terms of employment and would help to curb the insurgency problem to a minimal extent. One can also approach the government to allow them to take up contracts of maintaining the cleanliness and standards of the already existing tourist spots and develop it to such an extent to make it more marketable. There is a reason why in spite of so many tourist spots it is virtually impossible to market them due to lack of maintenance.

Role of Government in Tourism Development

The state mechanism needs to come up with industry oriented policies to boost the sector by granting incentives such as tax holiday and exemptions, etc. which will act as a leapfrog for the sector in the state. States like Nagaland and Sikkim do not impose luxury tax on hotels and VAT on food sales. Such has been done in order to promote tourism in their state. The government should try to adopt such initiatives followed by other states for the benefit of the local people. As per the NEIIPP 2007 Policy, two or above star category hotels are being treated as industry and subsidy has been granted on such initiatives. The onus is on the government to highlight such schemes to public and make them aware of various government benefits through media like television, radio, newspapers etc. Such incentives also act as a boost to attract young entrepreneurs to take initiatives. Further, the government also needs to ensure that the employees are well trained and possess thorough knowledge to help public in delivery of any scheme related queries.

It is observed that the employees have not been encouraged to take part in any of the training programmes on the pretext of insufficient funds in the department. Consequently, employees are also unaware of the schemes. Unexplored new tourist spots coupled with adventure sports will be a great success as the state is endowed with myriad topographical features. The government should develop the hitherto unexplored tourist places to a marketable level and try to maintain the same.

If at all the government fails to maintain the standards, then it should be handed over to private parties on lease and should assign the responsibility of marketing such tourist spots with them. Positive marketing should always be for the safety and convenience of the tourists. It is also observed that various government initiated tourism programmes are not attended by the grassroots level people who can exactly deliver the valuable information of the current prevailing scenario. The government has been swift in implementing schemes for tourism infrastructure development projects including mega projects worth crores of rupees. However, there is minimal or no proper implementation of various other grassroots level schemes which are equally important for overall tourism development in the State.

Why is Entrepreneurship the Key?

Emergence of an entrepreneur seeks to answer all the problems related with tourism. As we know, entrepreneurship is essentially a creative and an innovative activity. In regard to tourism, the following may be considered to know its exact importance.

Introduction of New Ideas: As mentioned earlier, the concept of village tourism and home stay are yet to be improvised despite its great demand. Introducing a traditional Manipuri *thali* would also add its value during the home stay. Arranging a special economy tour package is also a must for attracting the tourists.

Introduction of New Tourist Spots: Local entrepreneurs developing gardens and eco-parks have created a more conducive environment, highlighting the natural beauty of the state. Citing an example would be Kakching Uyok Garden, eco-park at Baruni Makhong, Millennium Garden etc.

Pooling of Human Resources: With the birth of the Classic Hotel, locals who worked outside the state have finally come back to their native place as their level of occupation has been maintained in the state itself. Such initiatives surely prevent the drain of human resources outside the state.

Creation of a New Organization for Industry: It has become a necessity for the formation of an association of the group of hotels in Manipur to approach the government for upliftment of state tourism. Such association will have more impact in influencing the government decisions.

Innovative Marketing: Local entrepreneurs can also be entrusted with the responsibility of bringing up a whole new level of marketing in the state tourism. A tie up with other North-Eastern states will have an enormous impact in promoting tourism as a whole.

Right Investments: Unlike government, the investment pattern in any enterprise would be valued accordingly and a proper financial discipline should be maintained which is vital in order to know the efficiency of the operations.

Conclusion

The kind of development that is unfolding in tourism needs careful consideration. Tourism department in order to thrive needs to encourage entrepreneurship among the locals to venture into new enterprises to promote state tourism. Encouraging private parties on PPP model would also bring the right initiatives from the government in order to reinvent the lost cause.

The basic ingredients of entrepreneurship such as creativity, innovations, and new ideas will definitely be able to bring a positive change in the current scenario. Thus, participation and emergence of local entrepreneurs holds the key in successful promotion of tourism in the state by expanding more markets and product profiles. However, just to be innovative is not enough unless that innovation is translated into action to promote state tourism and bring more number of tourists in the state.

References

Gajananda, Khwairakpam (2013), "Prospects and Problems of Look East Policy in Manipur', available at: http://kanglaonline.com/2013/12/prospects-and-problems-of-look-east-policy-in-manipur, accessed on May 30, 2014.

Imphal Free Press, (2014), "What Happened at the Eco-Tourism Conclave and What after This", Soraisam Devajani.

Industrial Policy of Manipur, 1996.

Industrial and Investment Policy of Manipur, 2013.

Singha, Challenges of Entrepreneurship Development in Manipur, available at: http://www.ukessays.com/essays/economics/challenges-of-entrepreneurship-development-in-manipur-economics-essay.php, accessed on May 30, 2014.

13

Entrepreneurial Finance

Mriganka Chakraborty

Introduction

Finance is the lifeblood of an enterprise. Financing constraints are one of the biggest concerns impacting the potential entrepreneurs around the world. Academic literature has focused on understanding several dimensions of financing constraints (Kerr and Nanda, 2009). The proper financing will definitely facilitate a vibrant industrial sector in any region. Finance is the key input of production, distribution and development and is a pre-requisite for accelerating the process of industrial development. The industrial finance relates to the financial institutions those provide financial resources for the conduct of industrial activities (Berger and Udell, 2004). It has been a well-known postulate that the Government of India pursued the policy of rapid industrialization corresponding to the process of socio-economic advancement of the country. Economic development of a region to a large extent depends on proper financing and capital plays a decisive role in determining the level of industrialization (Srinivas, 2005).

Tea is a customary drink in India which was first discovered in 2737 BC. In 1833, the East India Company after losing its legal monopoly of tea trade between China and Britain began to look for other routes of supply. As a result, the cultivation of tea in India began in 1834 (The History of Tea, 2003).

Over the years, tea has emerged as a favourite drink in the northern, eastern and western parts of India, unlike in the southern region where coffee is a major drink. It holds its supremacy of being a foreign exchange earner and supports the country's economy. India is the world's market leader in the tea segment, contributing about 31 percent of the global production (Veni, 2009). Indian tea exports have been an important foreign exchange earner for the country. There has been an inherent growth in export earnings from tea over the years. The Tea Board of India has been playing an important role in the field of tea plantation and research in India. In addition, financial grant in the form of research projects, subsidy and financial schemes for the tea entrepreneurs, etc. are also being provided to various other national institutes and universities for conducting tea research useful for the industry. Funds are also provided for organizing training programmes, seminars, conferences, workshops etc. to address the regional problems and provide solutions for the same.

Review of Related Literature

There have been a number of studies conducted on tea and entrepreneurship. A few studies in this context are highlighted in the following paragraphs.

Awasthi (1975) identified various additional facilities and fringe benefits provided by the management of tea gardens towards the workers. He also stated that multiplicity of taxes on tea had been a long standing grievance of the industry. He also presented a detailed picture of Assam tea industry relating to profitability and capital structure.

Viswanathan (1994) studied the working capital finance of tea gardens. He concluded that working capital limits to large tea borrowers should be fixed by banks purely on the basis of cash budgets and banks should desist themselves from financing tea brokers to enable them to lend to tea factories/ estates. Raul (1997) examined nature and problems of financing of industries including tea sector. He observed that owing to shortage of funds, fixed assets are being financed partly from long-term borrowings. The study hinted that financial assistance should be made available to these industries to meet the financial requirements. He also highlighted that the increasing cost of production, poor price realisation, etc. being the major impeding factors of profitability.

Petersen and Rajan (1997) found that the ratios of accounts payable and accounts receivable to sales are significantly higher for large firms than that of small business in the US. Hughes (1997) studied the trends of the financing of smaller businesses in UK. The study referred in particular to the findings of a major programme of work in the area funded by the Economic and Social Research Council and concluded that the evidence for general equity or debt gaps in the UK is weak. It was argued that consideration could be given to the promotion through seed-corn funding of SME co-operatives or mutual guarantee schemes to reduce information asymmetry in UK credit markets.

Sukarchakia (1999) and Mohan (1995) studied the inconvenience of Darjeeling tea. The most important problem related to the absence of quality control in Indian tea. Substandard teas are blended with Darjeeling tea and marketed as Darjeeling tea and as a result people are apprehensive of buying it with a high price. The cost of production of Darjeeling tea is high and people are ready to buy it at a high price. But it is a fact that average annual production in Darjeeling is around 10 to 11 million kg. only. But, about 40 million kg. of tea is marketed as Darjeeling tea in the world market. Other problems of tea in Darjeeling are over age of plants and fading productivity.

Ahmed (2000) in his paper entitled, "Factor Market Dualism, Small Scale Industry and Labour Absorption" took a closer look at the dualistic nature of labour and credit markets in developing countries in so far as their functioning is relevant for labour absorption in small-scale industry. He also quoted that institutional finance plays a minor role in capital needs of small-scale industry. Self-finance through personal savings, retained earnings, and family loans contribute 50-60 percent of capital needs of small and medium enterprises in developing countries. Bank financing becomes important as firms grow larger, but their role in financing initial investment remains minimal. The paper concluded that segmentation in labour and credits in developing countries is asymmetric in its implications for labour absorption in small-scale industry. Moreover, the high cost of capital and its unavailability to small scale is a serious constraint.

Atkotiya (2005) examined the financial performance of some selected tea companies in India from 1997-98 to 2002-03. He used a number of financial ratios to appraise the performance of the tea companies. He analysed the variance through Kruskal Wallis test. Based on the study, he concluded that profitability of the tea companies had been decreasing over the years and there had been wide variations in the financial structure of the companies. He also suggested that the companies should increase the production so as to get economies of the large-scale production which will assist in raising the rate of return on capital employed. In order to increase the profitability of the companies, it is suggested to control the cost of goods sold and operating expenses. The management should try to adopt cost reduction techniques in their companies to get over this critical situation. The quantum of sales generated should be improved impressively in order to promote better capital turnover ratio and to enjoy higher returns on investments.

Haldar (2004) studied the impact of entrepreneurial dynamics of small tea growers in rural transformation of Tripura. He observed that small tea grower's scheme reduces the mounting pressure on land on the one hand and provides ample opportunities for marginal and small farmers in rural Tripura on the other.

Hussain and Hazarika (2010) analysed the crisis of tea industry of Assam. According to their study, a considerable number of tea gardens of the State had gone sick over the period due to lack of infrastructure, modernization and efficient management. Chakraborty (2012) made a study on the profitability of tea gardens in the Barak Valley of Assam. It was revealed from the study that tea gardens in that region were sustaining losses due to increase in cost, decrease in average auction prices of Barak Valley tea and mounting burden of tax (cess and excise duty) on tea. Pandey and Ansari (2012) conducted a study on the role of financial institutions in the growth of women entrepreneurship. They urged that with the increasing role of women in economic development, it is required to stimulate educated young women into entrepreneurial streams with financial, technical and scientific assistance.

Hence, an incorporated approach is indispensable for making the progress of women entrepreneurship a success. Governmental and non-governmental organizations should be more focused and should initiate specific programmes for women entrepreneurship development. The EDPs and MDPs can become a crucial bond for harnessing immense and unexploited human skills to channelize them towards accelerating the gender mainstreaming and positioning women entrepreneur at par with men entrepreneurs.

Statement of the Problem

Till 1970s, UK was the major buyer of Indian tea. Since 1980s' USSR became the largest buyer of Indian tea due to existence of the trade agreement between India and the erstwhile USSR. USSR happened to be the major buyer of Indian tea accounting for more than 50 percent of the total Indian exports till 1991. However, with the disintegration of USSR and the abolition of Central Buying Mechanism, Indian tea exports suffered a setback from 1992-93.

However, Indian tea exports to Russian countries recovered from the setback since 1993 under the Rupee Debt Repayment Route facilities as also due to long-term agreement on tea entered into between Russia and India. Depressed scenario again started since 2001 due to change in the consumption pattern. Another reason for decline in export of

Indian tea to Russia was the offering of tea at lower prices by China and South Asian countries like Indonesia and Vietnam (ITC, 2003). Tea entrepreneurs in the Barak Valley were passing through a difficult terrain due to decrease in the average auction prices of tea over the last two decades because of the adoption of liberalized trade policy by the Government of India. Also, due to the sudden increase in the cost of production of tea, it has been invariably causing the decline in the profits of the tea entrepreneurs (ITA, 2005).

The establishment of tea garden requires huge investment with long gestation period. Equity capital forms only a small portion of the total investment. The rest has to be raised through loans from the financial institutions. The debt to equity ratio of tea plantations was 6.8 percent in 2004-05 which barely declined to 2.4 percent in 2006-07 and then again increased to 3.6 percent in 2008-09. As a result, the external source of funds to total sources of funds stood at 76.5 percent in 2008-09 (RBI, 2009). It is established that the loans provided to tea gardens for the planting of tea and its maintenance per unit of land was inadequate. With the present financing available, it may not be encouraging for small tea farmers to take up tea cultivation. Most of the tea planters have complained about the bureaucratic delays while availing credit facilities from the financial intuitions. Interest rates are high and the grace period provided is not enough.

Objectives of the Study

Hence, with the aforesaid background, the present study has been attempted to find out the quantum of credit granted by banks to tea entrepreneurs, sources of finance of tea entrepreneurs, purpose of obtaining institutional loans and the problems faced by the tea entrepreneurs in obtaining institutional finance.

Research Methodology

Sample Frame: Research population of the study

comprised of all the tea entrepreneurs operating in the study area. Sick gardens have remained outside the purview of the study. As on March 2013, there were 99 numbers of tea gardens (Tea Board records, Regional Office, Cachar) excluding sick gardens, scattered in three districts of the entire region under study. However, around 52 percent of the population i.e., a sample of 52 numbers of tea gardens were selected in a stratified random sampling basis for the purpose of the study.

Data Collection: Both primary and secondary data have been used for the purpose of the study. The sources of secondary data were Tea Board, Kolkata, Indian Tea Association, Surma Valley Branch, lead bank offices of the districts, regional offices of the scheduled commercial banks (SCBs), various reports, surveys, published and unpublished research papers and dissertations etc. The survey-cum-interview method has been used to assess the various sources of financing mix of tea gardens in the districts under study. The direct and personal interview was conducted to collect the relevant information which includes interview with proprietors and managers of tea gardens.

Findings and Discussions

Tea Financing by Banks in the Country: In Table 13.1, deployment of gross bank credit for the tea entrepreneurs in the country along with other industries is presented.

Table 13.1 reveals that the deployment of bank credit towards the tea industry has been a meagre percentage when compared with other industries. Also, the percentage of credit deployment towards the tea industry has been decreasing over the years. Again, the growth rate of bank finance towards tea industry has been 6.61 percent and in case of other industries, it has been 17.20 percent. Thus, the quantum of bank credit has been discouraging in case of the tea industry.

In this context, it has been confirmed by most of the sample units in the study area that most of the sample entrepreneurs were financed by the United Bank of India (UBI). Hence, in this section, an attempt has been made to highlight the scenario of financial assistance made by the UBI in the study area along with an all-India comparison and Assam.

Table 13.1: Deployment of Gross Bank Credit to Tea Industry (1990-2011)

Year	Tea Industry (₹ crore)	Other Industries (₹ crore)
1990	571 (0.51)	1,11,669
1991	608 (0.47)	1,28,228
1992	658 (0.49)	1,35,670
1993	782 (0.48)	1,63,618
1994	922 (0.55)	1,67,202
1995	1,106 (0.52)	2,12,408
1996	1,313 (0.50)	2,61,258
1997	814 (0.28)	2,89,748
1998	1,028(0.30)	3,40,796
1999	825 (0.22)	3,82,459
2000	1,034 (0.25)	4,29,097
2001	1,058 (0.22)	4,71,055
2002	986 (0.20)	4,98,315
2003	1,052 (0.16)	6,47,802
2004	1,222 (0.18)	6,95,776
2005	1,627 (0.17)	9,69,020
2006	1,851 (0.15)	12,64,675
2007	2,340 (0.15)	15,85,665
2008	2,483 (0.13)	19,50,115
2009	2,731 (0.11)	24,05,949
2010	1,995 (0.07)	30,25,438
2011	2,368 (0.06)	38,00,507
CAGR	6.61 %	17.20 %

Source: www.rbi.org.in. Figures within brackets indicate percentage to total.

Table 13.2 shows that the outstanding credit of UBI

towards tea entrepreneurs at the national level swelled from ₹ 268.89 crore in 2001 to ₹ 435.19 crore in 2013 whereas in the case of Assam and Barak Valley, the amount of outstanding credit grew from ₹ 174.23 crore in 2001 to ₹ 261.37 crore in 2013 and from ₹ 6.18 crore in 2001 to ₹ 6.99 crore in 2013 respectively. The amount outstanding grew by 1.62 times at the national level whereas in case of Assam and Barak Valley, it enhanced by 1.50 times and 1.13 times respectively. The calculated CAGR in respect of outstanding credit was 3.93 percent for all-India, 3.29 percent for Assam and 1.00 percent for Barak Valley. Thus, the CAGR in respect of outstanding credit of UBI towards tea industry has been highest at the national level.

Table 13.2: Outstanding Credit of United Bank of India towards Tea Industry

Year	All-India (₹ crore)	Assam (₹ crore)	Barak Valley (₹ crore)
2001	268.89	174.23	6.18
2002	288.72	194.23	6.41
2003	339.25	227.65	6.38
2004	366.26	241.08	8.14
2005	367.92	222.23	7.89
2006	381.89	240.64	6.97
2007	377.52	253.65	6.67
2008	366.89	253.90	3.74
2009	259.19	171.31	1.17
2010	263.98	170.36	6.98
2011	273.96	176.61	7.37
2012	359.48	227.17	6.19
2013	435.19	261.37	6.99
CAGR (%)	3.93	3.29	1.00

Source: Tea Department, United Bank of India, Kolkata.

In order to assess the extent of credit channelization by the UBI in the districts under study, we have calculated the correlation coefficients among the advances of UBI during 2001-2013 (Table 13.3).

Table 13.3: Matrix of Correlation Coefficient of Outstanding Credit of UBI

	All-India	Assam	Barak Valley
All-India	1		
Assam	0.9612 (11.39)*	1	
Barak Valley	0.3313 (1.3413)**	0.2333 (0.8846)**	1

Source: Self-calculated by the present researcher on the basis of previous table.

$t_{0.05}$(11 df) =1.796, $t_{0.01}$(11 df) =2.718

*indicates significant both at 0.05 and 0.01 level of significance.

**indicates insignificant both at 0.05 and 0.01 level of significance

The analysis reveals that correlation coefficient (r) in respect of outstanding credit of UBI in Assam and in the context of national scenario was positive. But the r values were not statistically significant for area under study. This implies that the area under study was not maintaining the national and state tempo of credit channelization by UBI. In other words, UBI was also not adequately deploying credit for the growth of tea industry when compared with credit deployment in the state level and national level.

Tea Board Financial Schemes

The Tea Board of India has been playing an important role in the field of tea plantation and research in India. Two major tea research institutes are located in the North-East region. These are the 'Darjeeling Tea Research and Development Centre' (DTR&DC) under the Tea Board, Kurseong, West Bengal, and 'Tea Research Association' (TRA) managed by the private sector at Jorhat, Assam. These institutes are involved in conducting basic and applied research required for the growth and development of Indian tea industry in general and the region specific problems of the industry. The following five schemes as indicated in Table 13.4 were approved for implementation during the Eleventh Five Year

Plan period (From April 1, 2007 to March 31, 2012).

Table 13.4: Schemes Approved for Implementation during the Eleventh Five Year Plan (2007-2011)

S. No.	Name of the Scheme	Approved Outlay (₹ crore)		10th Plan Expenditure (₹ crore)
		11th Plan	10th Plan	
1.	Tea Plantation Development Scheme (TPDS)	316	98.59	112.85
2.	Quality Upgradation and Product Diversification Scheme (QUPDS)	230	76.80	64.64
3.	Market Promotion Scheme (MPS)	119	98.60	90.53
4.	Research and Development Scheme (R&D)	85	70.00	79.72
5.	Human Resource Development Scheme (MPS)	50	6.01	5.69
	Total for regular schemes	800	350.00	353.43
6.	Other ad hoc schemes	6.43*	146.25**	106.45**
	Total Budgetary Support	806.43	496.25	459.88

Source: 54th Annual Report, Tea Board.

* ₹ 6.43 crore (US$ 1.60 million) to be received over next three years from Common Fund for Commodities (CFC) on account of Organic Tea Development Project

** The ad-hoc schemes sanctioned during the 10th Plan.

These schemes were implemented during the Tenth Plan period as well have been approved for continuation during the Eleventh Plan period with certain modifications and higher outlays. These are:

- Orthodox production incentive scheme: ₹ 65.00 crore
- Additional support to R&D institutions: ₹ 28.00 crore
- Price subsidy scheme for small growers: ₹ 23.25 crore
- Capital contribution to SPTF Fund: ₹ 30.00 crore
- Total sanction: ₹ 146.25 crore

Table 13.4 shows that highest amount sanctioned during the 10th plan period was under TPDS followed by MPS and R&D scheme. Moreover, the highest amount approved for the 11th plan was also for TPDS followed by QUPDS, MPS, etc.

Sources of Finance of Sample Units

The role of institutional finance is a prime requirement for industrial development of any region. The availability of finance to the tea entrepreneurs with reference to types of financial institutions is presented in Table 13.5.

Table 13.5: Availability of Finance to Sample Units

S. No.	Types of Financial Institutions	Number of Tea Gardens	Percent to Total
1.	Institutional Finance	44	84.63
A	SCBs and Tea Board	33	63.47
B	Assam Cooperative Apex Bank and Tea Board	5	9.62
C	Tea Board	2	3.85
D	NABARD and Tea Board	4	7.69
2.	Tea Board and Body Corporates	7	13.47
3.	Self Finance/No Finance	1	1.90
Total		52	100

Source: Field Survey.

Data compiled from the field survey shows that the sample tea gardens have been mostly relying on institutional financing for re-plantation, extension, installation of machinery and other short-term and long-term financial requirements. It reveals that 98.10 percent of the sample units had outstanding loans from all sources, whereas 84.63 percent of the units had outstanding loans from institutional sources and 13.47 percent units had taken loans from Tea Board and body corporate. Thus, while 44 numbers of units had access to institutional sources of finance, only 1 unit relied upon self-finance. Out of the sample tea gardens surveyed, only one tea garden was found to have not resorted to any sort of external financing over the study period. We also found from the field investigation that out of the total institutional borrowers under the head SCBs and Tea Board, about 70 percent of them had outstanding towards United Bank of India and the remaining 30 percent had outstanding towards other banks. This leads us to a further enquiry for the purpose for which loan was used.

Purpose of Loan and Credit

The preceding analysis found that out of 52 numbers of sample tea gardens, only 44 numbers of units had taken loan from institutional sources. To know the purpose of credit/loan taken, we have presented the collected data in Table 13.6.

Table 13.6: Purpose of Loan/Credit

S. No.	Purpose	Number of Respondents	Percentage
1.	To extend the area of plantation	14	28.00
2.	Modernisation of plant	10	19.60
3.	Increase in working capital only	11	21.56
4.	Increase in production capacity/and increase in working capital	8	17.31
5.	Extension, irrigation, transportation, etc.	8	17.31
Total		51	100.00

Source: Field Survey.

Table 13.6 clearly reveals that only 28 percent of tea gardens obtained institutional credit to extend the area of plantation. We also came to know from the investigation that those who obtained institutional credit to extend the area of plantation, was actually financed under Tea Board subsidy/ loan scheme. For 21.56 percent of the respondents, the loan was extended for increase in the working capital. Regards the finance for increase in production capacity/working capital, around 50 percent of the cases utilized it for working capital only. Extension, irrigation and transportation accounted for nearly 17.31 percent out of which around 56 percent was marked for extension and irrigation.

Problems Faced by the Tea Entrepreneurs

The tea entrepreneurs faced diverse inconvenience while obtaining finance from financial institutions including the Tea Board. We tried to examine the problems of sample units on the basis of their response provided in the schedules. Six (6) strictures each influencing for getting loans/credit were identified as: (i) security and collateral, (ii) delay in sanction, (iii) high interest rate, (iv) heavy documentation, (v) decrease in auction prices and profitability, and (vi) other reasons based on observation of the researcher and in consultation with the sample entrepreneurs.

The opinion of the respondents i.e., tea garden entrepreneurs was sought based on the rank of the nature of problems from 1st to 6th with regards to the strength of the parameters. A score of 5,4,3,2,1 and 0 were given to ranks 1st, 2nd, 3rd, 4th, 5th and 6th respectively. The frequencies of respondents ranking against each problem in each rank was calculated (by multiplying the corresponding score value) to obtain the total score values. The problem with highest score value was considered as more harsh followed by reasons with decreasing order of score values. Table 13.7 evidences the result of the analysis.

It is perceptible from the above analysis that the major problems encountered by tea entrepreneurs for getting loans was the decrease in auction prices and profitability as it had got the highest score of 228. This was followed by security and collateral (score 196), other reasons (score 192), heavy documentation (score 180), delay in sanction (178), and high interest rate (score 143).

Table 13.7: Problems Faced in Raising Finance from Financial Institutions

Nature of the Problem	Rank 1, score 5		Rank 2, score 4		Rank 3, score 3	
	No. of units	Total score	No. of units	Total score	No. of units	Total score
1. Security and collateral	18	90	15	60	11	33
2. Delay in sanction	15	75	14	56	11	33
3. High interest rate	11	55	19	38	10	30
4. Heavy documentation	9	45	18	72	13	39
5. Decrease in auction prices and profitability	30	150	14	56	6	18
6. Other reasons	21	105	10	40	9	27
Total	104		90		60	

Contd...

Nature of the Problem	Rank 4, score 2		Rank 5, score 1		Rank 6, score 0	
	No. of units	Total score	No. of units	Total score	No. of units	Total score
1. Security and collateral	5	10	3	3	0	0
2. Delay in sanction	5	10	4	4	3	0
3. High interest rate	8	16	4	4	0	0
4. Heavy documentation	12	24	0	0	0	0
5. Decrease in auction prices and profitability	2	4	0	0	0	0
6. Other reasons	8	16	4	4	0	0
Total	40		15		3	

Contd...

Nature of the Problem	Total
1. Security and Collateral	196
2. Delay in sanction	178
3. High interest rate	143
4. Heavy documentation	180
5. Decrease in auction prices and profitability	228
6. Other reasons	192
Total	1119

Source: Field Survey.

This indicates that reducing auction prices and profitability was the biggest hurdle in obtaining finance. An urgent step in this direction is indispensable to ensure a sound price and higher profit margins for the tea gardens in the region along with necessary steps to reduce the cost of production.

Concluding Observations

For the proper development of tea entrepreneurs, a number of policies have to be evolved to solve various problems pertaining to the financing of the tea entrepreneurs. The slice of entrepreneurship is very much significant for positioning of research on financing constriction. Developing a proper mechanism for developing entrepreneurship is an important goal for many governments, and researchers need to define for policy makers a more unified perspective for how studies and samples fit together. The banks should also review and further revise the system of collateral provision. There is also a need for better coordination between financial institutions and tea entrepreneurs.

References

Ahmed, J. (2000), "Factor Market Dualism, Small Scale Industry and Labour Absorption", *Journal of Economic Development*, Vol. 25, Number 1, June 2000.

Atkotiya, Kanak N. (2005), "Analysis of Financial Performance of Tea Industry in India", Ph.D. thesis, Saurashtra University, Gujarat.

Awasthi, R.C. (1975), "Economics of Tea Industry in India", United Publishers, Guwahati.

Berger and Udell (2004), "Small Business Finance in the 21st Century", in Office of Advocacy, Entrepreneurship in the 21st Century: Conference Proceedings, March 26, 2004, available at: http://www.sba.gov/advo/stats/proceedings_a.pdf, accessed on July 23, 2009.

Chakraborty, M. (2012), "Profitability of Tea Gardens: A Study in the Barak Valley Region of Assam", in *Source, A Peer Reviewed Journal of Humanities and Social Sciences,* Vol. II, pp. 123-133.

Haldar, P.K. (2004) "Study of the Impact of Entrepreneurial Dynamics of Small Tea Growers in Rural Transformation of Tripura", in Ahmed, J.U. (ed.), Industrialization in N.E. Region,

Mittal Publications, New Delhi.

Hughes, Alan (1997), "Finance for SMEs: A U.K. Perspective", *Small Business Economics*, Springer Netherlands, 9(2): 151-168, April.

Hussain, M.M. and Hazarika, S.D. (2010), "Assam Tea Industry and its Crisis", *Dialogue,* July-September, Vol. 12, No. 1.

Indian Tea Association (2005), "Tea Statistics", Kolkata.

International Tea Committee (2003), Annual Bulletin of Statistics, London.

Kerr, William. R. and Nanda, R. (2009), "Financing Constraints and Entrepreneurship", *Harvard Business School,* Working Paper.

Mohan, Sushil (1995), "Darjeeling Tea: Is It Really from Darjeeling", *Tea International, The Journal of World Tea Trade,* Vol. 3, Issue 2, No. 9.

Pandey, N. and Ansari, M.A. (2012), "Role of Financial Institutions in the Development of Women Entrepreneurship", *Indian Research Journal of Extension Education,* Vol. I, January.

Petersen, Mitchell and Raghuram Rajan (1994), "The Benefits of Firm-creditor Relationships: Evidence from Small-business Data", *Journal of Finance*, 49, 3-37.

Raul, R.K. (1997), "Industrial Finance in India", Anmol Publications, New Delhi.

Srinivas, Y. (2005), "Bank Finance to the SME Sector: Issues and Perspectives", *The Chartered Accountant*, September, pp. 436-439.

Sukarchakia, I.S. (1999), "Darjeeling Tea", *Contemporary Tea Time,* Vol. III, No. 2, June-August.

Veni, L.K. (2009), "India as Top Producer of Tea in the World: Some Observations", in Sen, S. (ed.) Global Tea Industry: Some Reflections, ICFAI University Press, Hyderabad, pp. 58-77.

14

Socio-economic Impact of Tourism Entrepreneurship

Benjamin F. Lyngdoh

Introduction

The creation of a country's wealth and its dynamism depends upon the competitiveness of its firms which in turn relies fundamentally on the capabilities of its entrepreneurs (Cuervol, Ribeiro and Roig, 2008). The term entrepreneur is French and is derived from the verb *entreprendre* which means *to do* or *to undertake*. It is divided into two parts–*entre* meaning *between* and *preneur* meaning *taker*. Hence, an *entrepreneur* is a *between-taker* or a *go-between* (Filion, 2011). Apart from many others, leading definitions define entrepreneur as one who predicts and acts upon change within markets and bears the uncertainty of market dynamics (Knight, 1921) and an innovator who implements change within markets through the carrying out of new combinations (Schumpeter, 1934).

Synthesizing on the many resources available on the subject matter, an all encompassing definition is derived. As such, an entrepreneur is that person (business owner) who seeks to generate value through the creation or expansion of economic activity by identifying and exploiting new products, processes and markets. In addition, entrepreneurial activity is the enterprising human action in pursuit of the generation of value through the creation or expansion of economic activity by identifying and exploiting new products, processes or markets. Accordingly, entrepreneurship is the phenomenon associated with entrepreneurial activity (Ahmad and Seymour, 2008).

Entrepreneurship is a dynamic function and envelopes a plethora of managerial aspects. As such, it is a field of study under management discipline (Busenitz, et al., 2003). It involves a range and depth of functions which are ultimately aimed at value creation for utility to the consumers. It is highly influenced by the business environment. As the enterprises are mainly micro and small, they do not possess the strength to dictate the environment. On the contrary, their roles, functions and profitability are clearly defined by the progress of the economy. Conversely, one form of such entrepreneurship as per classification of *focus* and *operations* is tourism entrepreneurship.

Tourism is defined as 'the activities of persons travelling to and staying in places outside their usual environment for not more than one consecutive year for leisure, business and other purposes' (World Tourism Organisation [WTO], 1995). It is the most attractive and the fastest growing industry in the world (Othman and Rosli, 2011). Unlike many other sectors, tourism is unable to be defined simply as a group of businesses that produce products, but, it embraces a diverse range of providers and users of a variety of goods and services and overlaps with other sectors of the economy (Coetzer, 2001/02). As such, the range of activities under the umbrella of tourism has been in perennial existence and growing continuously. According to the Online Etymology Dictionary, the word 'tourist' and 'tourism' first appeared in 1780 and 1811 respectively.

Since then, the sector has grown considerably and encompassed directly or indirectly effects on the progress and development of various fronts such as economic, social, political, cultural, overall national development and international relations (Ashley, 2000; Brida, Carrera and Risso, 2008; Fayissa, Nsiah and Tadasse, 2007; Goodwin, 2006; Vellas, 2011; WTO, 1995; World Travel and Tourism Council [WTTC], 2006, 2012; Zortuk, 2009).

In the tourism sector, all entrepreneurship focuses upon the tourist clientele and running operations accordingly can be classified as tourism entrepreneurship. It is a phenomenon that is flourished by current economic, social and political conditions in a particular destination and highly depends on both the closed and far environment (Aghapour, Hojabri, Manafi and Hosseini, 2012). Tourism entrepreneurship includes activities related to creating and operating a legal tourist enterprise and refers to those businesses that operate on a profitable basis and seek to satisfy the needs of tourists and visitors. As such, persons and businesses that hawk goods or services such as arts and crafts to tourists are tourism entrepreneurs (Koh, 1996). It has been identified as essential actors for creating jobs and generally growing the economy (Taskov, Metodijeski, Dzaleva and Filipovski, 2011) with continuous efforts on innovations such as process, management, logistical and institutional (Hjalager, 2002).

In general, tourism entrepreneurship is manifest in the form of guide services, small spa and massage facilities, specialized bakery and pastry shops, coffee shops, souvenir trading and crafts shops, travel agencies, small tour operators, small lodges rented, lodges, small hotels, larger restaurants, recreation businesses, bus companies and so forth including others like taxi drivers, food and beverage producers, trading shops, pharmacies, photocopy shops and so forth (Sterren, 2008).

Globally, the tourism sector is dominated by micro enterprises and the self-employed (Oldbell, 2007). In India, the sector has a strong presence of micro and small enterprises (Indian Institute of Tourism and Travel Management, 2010). This is understandable as the businesses engaged in tourism, mainly involves providing and rendering services which can be handled by micro enterprises (Tourism and Transport Consult International, 2011).

In general, they have been identified as the most viable business structure to fight poverty and kick-start development, consistent with the sustainable livelihoods approach to rural poverty reduction (Shen, Hughey and Simmons, 2008) with the tourism sector being no exception to the rule (Manyara and Jones, 2007).

Accordingly, the present study aims to explore the socio-economic impact of tourism entrepreneurship in a global context through a focus on micro and small enterprises. The method adopted involves an extensive review of documented sources and systematically highlights such impact. Consequently, in addition to the introduction, the study is classified into additional parts. The additional parts portray the socio-economic impact of tourism entrepreneurship and present issues of impact and pens down the conclusion.

Socio-economic Impact

Globally, tourism has experienced continued expansion and diversification overtime. More economies have identified tourism as one of the engines for growth and development. It has become one of the largest and high growing economic sectors. Further, the sector has the potential to provide jobs at all levels from restaurant staff and chambermaids in hotels to guides and taxi drivers as well as management in tourism enterprises and other related businesses. It is basically a labour-intensive, quality-driven service profession which depends crucially on the skill level and professionalism of the workforce for productivity and competitiveness (WTTC, 2006). Tourism is seen as an activity which affects society in many ways and has a profound impact on social, cultural and economic life (Coetzer, 2001/02).

For example, it has made a significant contribution to Botswana graduating away from least developed country status (the classification of least developed country was made in 1971). In addition, since 1994 there have been four potential graduation cases viz. Cape Verde, Maldives, Samoa and Vanuatu, in all of them, tourism has been the single most important factor explaining the socio-economic progress that would induce graduation (Encontre, 2001). Hence, for poor countries, regions, towns and cities, tourism is seen as a fast track to development (Mbaiwa, 2003).

Traditionally, the impact of tourism has been measured in terms of its contribution to gross national product and employment created (Jamieson, Goodwin and Edmunds, 2004) and the impacts of tourism can be sorted into seven general categories namely, economic, environmental, social and cultural, crowding and congestion, services, taxes and community attitude (Kreag, 2001). Tourism provides wide-ranging opportunities for foreign investors and local entrepreneurs.

It brings inward investment, foreign exchange earnings and creation of small, medium and micro businesses (Mshenga and Owuor, 2009). It has a direct and secondary effects on the economy, particularly in gross domestic product, tax revenue and sales value (Fayissa, et al., 2007; Flecha, Fusco, Damiani and Amaral, 2010), provides employment opportunities, generates supply of foreign exchange, increases income, improves infrastructure, creates favourite image of the country, provides recreational facilities for residents as well as tourists and so forth (Kim, 2002).

The adoption of Millennium Development Goals by the United Nations and other bilateral and multilateral development agencies has encouraged the World Tourism Organization, national tourism administrations and some development agencies to adopt new approaches to tourism development by focussing on local economic impacts and in particular on poverty alleviation (Goodwin, 2006).

Until recently, tourism development has not sought to demonstrate the impacts of tourism on poverty reduction as the focus has been on macro economic impact and its potential to bring economic growth to poor and marginalized individuals and communities (Jamieson, et al., 2004). In the context of Millennium Development Goals, the challenge is to demonstrate positive impacts on poverty and to demonstrate that tourism can contribute to all the eight goals (Goodwin, 2006). Overall, tourism can contribute to the goal of sustainable development as well as development of local economies if it is linked to the local economies. As such, in the recent past, focus in tourism has shifted to pro-poor tourism (Mshenga and Owuor, 2009).

Tourism exhibits impacts of economic nature through creation of small business opportunities which provide employment and earnings, creation of direct employment in formal sector businesses by the poor, development of collective benefits where a community gains from concession or lease agreements with formal sector enterprises or from user fees for passing through a village or visiting a community forest and charitable donations from tourism businesses or from tourists.

The impacts of non-economic nature include opportunities for capacity building, education and training, improvements in health, education and other forms of well-being, net positive environmental impacts which benefit the poor, improved socio-cultural status through community recognition and increased pride and self-confidence and reduced vulnerability through livelihood diversification. However, negative impacts are also present in the form of pressure on services and facilities necessitating increased investment, increased cost of living for local people, culture, local traditions and ways of life becoming a commodity, traditional residents being displaced, increased incidence in crime, increase in pollution and degradation of the environment (Jamieson, et al., 2004).

Globally, micro and small enterprises contribute to economic growth through the primary and secondary pathways that go beyond job creation. Primary pathways have greater and direct impact on growth and economic dynamism and secondary pathways are the indirect channels that contribute to overall economic growth and include human capital improvement, financial market development and so forth (Leegwater and Shaw, 2008). In India, they are well known for their contribution to industrial production, exports and employment (Ramarao, 2012). For tourism to be beneficial in terms of income generation, economic growth, poverty reduction and improving rural livelihoods, it has to be linked to local economies such as agriculture and micro and small enterprises (Mshenga and Owuor, 2009).

Tourism brings about a positive impact on the local economy and entrepreneurial development (Ashley, Roe and Goodwin, 2001; Othman and Rosli, 2011). The poor are involved in all the initiatives as individual producers, employees, casual labourers and operators of micro and small enterprises (Ashley, et al., 2001). High proportion of business enterprises come from the small sector (Awang, Aziz and Samdin, 2012). As such, tourism creates opportunities for small entrepreneurs because start-up costs for and barriers to entry are relatively low and can be accessible to the poor (Othman and Rosli, 2011; UNESCAP, 2005). Local people, including the poor, have opportunities to earn additional income by selling produce or offering services directly to tourists (UNESCAP, 2005). Tourism entrepreneurs contribute to raising productivity, dispersal of economic power base through industry ownership, creating employment, commercialising innovative products and creating new markets (Awang, et al., 2012).

On sustainable practice of micro and small enterprise, the impacts are mainly seen in socio-economic domains of the entrepreneurs (Kreag, 2001) amongst others. It provides employment, training, business skills and improves the socio-economic outcomes of families and communities. As the tourism sector is more labour-intensive, requiring a high proportion of unskilled or semi-skilled labour, it impacts upon the wages and earnings of entrepreneurs, livelihood strategies of local households, business climate for small enterprise development, patterns of growth of the local or national economy and the infrastructure or natural resource base of the destination (Ashley, Brine, Lehr and Wilde, 2007). Despite the importance of all the other impacts, there is no doubt that earning cash is the prime motivation for entrepreneurship (Ashley, 2000).

Similarly, the passion to achieve positive outcomes is a strong driver in the practice of enterprise (Rola-Rubzen, et al., 2011). They impact upon livelihood strategies through changes in employment and earnings, development of collective benefits in the community, capacity building; education and training, improvements in health and education, community recognition, increased pride and self-confidence and reduced vulnerability through livelihood diversification (Ashley, et al., 2007; Jamieson, et al., 2004). It results in appreciation in financial assets for investment, physical assets like livestock and agriculture, human skills like communication and coordination, social capital through trust and networks, regular wages/salary, profits from the enterprise, decreased household economic vulnerability, enhancement of food security, improvement in pride and empowerment through independent decision-making and gaining of recognition (Ashley, 2000).

Although, rigorous empirical national and global level analysis of tourism economics and poverty alleviation impact is lacking, nevertheless it is clear that the industry is having substantial influence on local people and local economies in many developing countries. In the 'best case' destinations, estimates show that earnings of local unskilled and semi-skilled people were equivalent to approximately a quarter of tourist spending at the destination level (Ashley, et al., 2007).

Despite growing evidence of the beneficial impacts of tourism in developing countries and good practices by some individual firms, critics still question whether the overall balance of impacts is positive (Ashley, et al., 2007). As such, an assessment of impact depends not only on direct costs and benefits such as profits and jobs generated but on a range of indirect, positive and negative impacts (Ashley, 2000). Tourism can have negative impacts like depriving local people of access to natural resources like fishing grounds, forests and water (Ashley, et al., 2007), inflation of land value, raising price on food, seasonal employment, displacement of labour, overcrowding and so forth (Kim, 2002).

Impact of Tourism Entrepreneurship: Some Issues

Despite the positives on the socio-economic impact of tourism, limited interest has been paid to the role of entrepreneurship particularly in relation to micro enterprise and very little literature is available on the subject-matter (Coetzer, 2001/02). Globally, research into tourism entrepreneurship role in socio-economic growth and development of entrepreneurs is somewhat limited, partial and fractional, has substantial gaps and is vastly under-researched (Dahles, 1999; Page and Getz, 1997; Shaw, 2004; Thomas, 2004; Tinsley and Lynch, 2001). Although, there has been a flourishing of interest in a variety of issues related to micro and small businesses in tourism, yet, this area of inquiry is vastly under-researched and the depth of our knowledge of the dynamics of smaller enterprises in tourism and how they articulate with the economy and society remains relatively shallow (Thomas, 2004; Tinsley and Lynch, 2001).

Research has tended to focus on larger non-service organisations with very little focus on the role of micro enterprises in the tourism sector (Coetzer, 2001/02). The impacts of tourism on a community are not widely understood (Kreag, 2001). There are very few cases where the poverty impacts of particular tourism initiatives have been researched or monitored and reported (Goodwin, 2006). Overall, the available literature is remarkably uninformative about the role and position of small and micro enterprises in the tourism industry (Coetzer, 2001/02). Hence, demonstrating the benefits of tourism in addressing poverty is a challenge (Goodwin, 2006).

In most impact evaluation studies, development impacts are too often equated with 'jobs and cash' particularly by planners, donors or conservationists. In such a situation, the livelihoods approach helps broaden the scope of analysis to a wide range of livelihood impacts. In doing so it seeks to reflect better the more complex reality of poor people's concerns and aspirations (Ashley, 2000). Moreover, there is an increasing interest in micro businesses and small entrepreneurs operating in the tourism industry. However, this is rather limited to that of developing countries and is related to investigations into the potential of sustainable development (Coetzer, 2001/02). Nonetheless, while the literature refers to the importance of tourism in the developing countries, rural and marginalized areas, there is very little consideration of the impact of tourism on the poor (Jamieson, et al., 2004). Hence, this gap in research presents an opportunity for venturing into. It presents the prospect for examining impacts at a micro/unit level thereby bringing to light the different facets of change in its totality.

It is beyond doubt that entrepreneurship is a contributor for the growth and development of any nation. They have a potential in both developed and developing countries as an engine for providing employment, inclusive growth, exports and innovation. However, the contribution of this sector to the economy is dependent upon the competitiveness and sustainability of the firms (Ramarao, 2012). Impacts will have less bearing in the absence of long-term sustainability. Hence, a focus has to be laid upon this perspective. In general and with particular reference to developing countries, there are four conventional perspectives on tourism. The economists see tourism as a route to macro-economic growth and a means of generating foreign exchange. The private sector view tourism as a commercial activity and as such the main concerns are product development, competitiveness and commercial returns. For the conservationists, tourism is a form of sustainable use of wild resources and hence a way to enhance incentives for conservation. For the rural people and the non-governmental organisations that support them, tourism is one component of rural development.

The last perspective places the interests of the poor at the centre as the livelihoods approach. It is used to develop the fourth perspective and to explore how development impacts can be expanded while recognising the continuing prevalence of the other three perspectives. Maximizing livelihood benefits needs a good understanding of what people most need and want (their livelihood priorities) and of the complex ways in which tourism options affect livelihoods (direct and indirect livelihood impacts).

Therefore, it requires a considerable role for local people in decision-making. This can be done either by devolving tourism rights to community level and helping communities with participatory planning or by ensuring that government planning processes are participatory and responsive to local needs or by ensuring through government incentives that planning by private entrepreneurs is responsive to local needs (Ashley, 2000). As such, this livelihood approach will be more appealing and significant if it embeds within it a feature of being sustainable. Hence, not just livelihood approach, but, focus should be on sustainable livelihoods approach.

In general, tourism development does employ those in the lower social and economic classes but there is a growing body of evidence that tourism development enriches local elites, international and expatriate companies and generates low paying and low status employment. As such, when assessing the positive impacts of tourism initiatives on the livelihoods and welfare of poor people, the analysis must also identify and report on any negative impacts which may result from such initiatives like loss of access to grazing or water, loss of access to beaches for fishing and so forth (Jamieson, et al., 2004).

This also highlights the importance of making tourism planning and development pro-poor. In general, tourism is pro-poor if it provides economic gain through the creation of full or part-time employment or the development of micro and small opportunities through sales to tourism businesses or to tourists, other livelihood benefits such as access to potable water, roads which bring benefits to poor producers through improved access to markets, improved health or education, opportunities and capacity for engagement in decision-making so that the poor are able to improve their livelihoods by securing better access to tourists and tourism enterprises.

Conclusion

The review of documented sources concerning the socio-economic impact of tourism entrepreneurship throws forward some interesting facts. Some are routine and expected whereas some are novel and presents the impact evaluation thinking in a paradigm shift. Tourism has grown and developed overtime and for most economies it is the largest and high growth sector. It contributes towards the socio-economic growth and development of both developed and developing economies at macro level.

In addition, it significantly adds to the range and depth of tourism entrepreneurship, manifest in the form of micro and small enterprises. This is possible because of the nature of the tourism sector whereby it creates myriad opportunities for such business. Moreover, despite limited empirical evidences, it is derived reasonably that tourism entrepreneurship does contribute towards the socio-economic outcomes of the entrepreneur. However, concerns over the negative impacts of tourism and tourism entrepreneurship do exist. These are to be mapped out and dealt with through a focus on sustainability of operations so as to ensure sustainable livelihoods through tourism.

As such, tourism impact evaluations should shift their approach towards broader development impacts through a focus on livelihoods. Moreover, such a livelihood approach should encompass sustainability as its core principle. This would ensure more tourism impacts which are sustainable. Hence, the paradigm thinking should be centred upon sustainable livelihoods approach. This requires tourism planning and development from the perspective of sustainable operations and processes and overall sustainability of the sector. Lastly, tourism planning should be based on the principle of being all inclusive and pro-poor as majority of people involved in tourism entrepreneurship belong to the bottom strata of the society.

References

Aghapour, A.H., Hojabri, R., Manafi, M. and Hosseini, S. (2012), "Behind Ambiguities of Tourism Entrepreneurship", *International Journal of Innovative Ideas,* 12(3), 25-29.

Ahmad, N. and Seymour, R.G. (2008), "Defining Entrepreneurial Activity: Definitions Supporting Frameworks for Data Collection", available at: http://www.oecd.org/officialdocuments/ publicdisplaydocumentpdf/?doclanguage=en&cote=std/doc.

Ashley, C. (2000), "The Impacts of Tourism on Rural Livelihoods: Namibia's Experience", available at: http://www.odi.org.uk/sites/odi.org.uk/files/odi-assets/publications-opinion-files/2754.pdf.

Ashley, C., Brine, P.D., Lehr, A. and Wilde, H. (2007), "The Role of the Tourism Sector in Expanding Economic Opportunity", Cambridge, MA: Kennedy School of Government, Harvard University.

Ashley, C., Roe, D. and Goodwin, H. (2001), "Pro-poor Tourism Strategies: Making Tourism Work for the Poor", London: Overseas Development Institute.

Awang, K.W., Aziz, Y.A. and Samdin, Z. (2012), "The Growth of Small Hotel Enterprises: The Roles of the State", International Proceedings of Economics Development and Research, 38, 145-49.

Brida, J.G., Carrera, E.J.S. and Risso, W.A. (2008), "Tourism's Impact on Long-run Mexican Economic Growth", *Economics Bulletin,* 3(21), 1-8.

Busenitz, L.W. West, G.P., Shepherd, D., Nelson, T., Chandler, G.N. and Zacharakis, A. (2003), "Entrepreneurship Research in Emergence: Past Trends and Future Directions, *Journal of Management*, 29, 285-308.

Coetzer, J. (2001/02), "Micro Enterprises: To Evaluate and Understand Tourism and Micro-sized Enterprises in a Perpetually Changing Environment", Ph.D. Bournemouth University.

Cuervol, A., Ribeiro, D. and Roig, S. (2008), "Entrepreneurship: Concepts, Theory and Perspective", available at: http://www.uv.es/bcjauveg/docs/LibroCuervoRibeiroRoigIntrod

uction.pdf.

Dahles, H. (1999), "Tourism and Small Entrepreneurs in Developing Countries: A Theoretical Perspective", in H. Dahles and K. Bras (eds.), Tourism and Small Entrepreneurs: Development, National Policy and Entrepreneurial Culture: Indonesian Cases, pp. 1-19, New York: Cognizant Communication Corporation.

Encontre, P. (2001), "Tourism Development and the Perspective of Graduation from the LDC Category", in World Tourism Organization and United Nations Conference on Trade and Development, Tourism in the Least Developed Countries, World Tourism Organization, Madrid.

Fayissa, B., Nsiah, C. and Tadasse, B. (2007), "The Impact of Tourism on Economic Growth and Development in Africa", available at:
http://capone.mtsu.edu/berc/working/TourismAfricawp.pdf.

Filion, L.J. (2011), "Defining the Entrepreneur", in L. Dana (ed.), World Encyclopaedia of Entrepreneurship, pp. 41-52, Cheltenham, UK and Northampton, MA: Edward Elgar.

Flecha, A.C., Fusco, J.P.A., Damiani, W.B. and Amaral, H.F. (2010), "The Economic Impacts of Tourism in Ouro Preto, MG, Brazil", *Brazilian Journal of Operations and Production Management,* 7(2), 29-46.

Goodwin, H. (2006), "Measuring and Reporting the Impact of Tourism on Poverty", available at:
http://www.www.bidnetwork.org/sites/default/files/measuring.pdf.

Hjalager, A.M. (2002), "Repairing Innovation Defectiveness in Tourism", *Tourism Management,* 23, 465-474.

Indian Institute of Tourism and Travel Management (2010), "Analyzing the Factors Responsible for Slowdown in Tourist Arrivals in India", New Delhi: Ministry of Tourism.

Jamieson, W., Goodwin, H. and Edmunds, C. (2004), "Contribution of Tourism to Poverty Alleviation: Pro-poor Tourism and the Challenge of Measuring impacts", available at:
http://haroldgoodwin.info/resources/povertyalleviation.pdf.

Kim, K. (2002), "The Effects of Tourism Impacts Upon Quality of Life of Residents in the Community", Ph.D. Virginia Polytechnic Institute and State University.

Knight, F.H. (1921), "Risk, Uncertainty and Profit", Chicago: University of Chicago Press.

Koh, K.Y. (1996), "The Tourism Entrepreneurial Process: A Conceptualization and Implications for Research and Development", *Tourism Review,* 51(4), 24-41.

Kreag, G. (2001), "The Impacts of Tourism", available at: http://www.seagrant.umn.edu/tourism /pdfs/ImpactsTourism.pdf

Leegwater, A. and Shaw, A. (2008), "The Role of Micro, Small and Medium Enterprises in Economic Growth: A Cross-country Regression Analysis", Washington D.C.: United States Agency for International Development.

Manyara, G. and Jones, E. (2007), "Community-based Tourism Enterprises Development in Kenya: An Exploration of their Potential as Avenues of Poverty Reduction", *Journal of Sustainable Tourism,* 15(6), 628-44.

Mbaiwa, J.E. (2003), "The Socio-economic and Environmental Impacts of Tourism Development on the Okavango Delta, North-western Botswana, *Journal of Arid Environments,* 54(2), 447-467.

Mshenga, P.M. and Owuor, G. (2009), "Opportunities for Micro and Small-scale Businesses in the Tourism Sector: The Case of the Kenya Coast", *KCA Journal of Business Management,* 2(2), 52-68.

Oldbell (2007), "Research into the Skill Needs and Requirements of the Hospitality, Leisure, Travel and Tourism Sectors", Report to Department for Children, Education, Lifelong Learning and Skills, Welsh Assembly Government, Wales, UK.

Othman, P. and Rosli, M.M. (2011), "The Impact of Tourism on Small Business Performance: Empirical Evidence from Malaysian Islands", *International Journal of Business and Social Science,* 2(1), 11-21.

Page, S.J. and Getz, D. (1997), "The Business of Rural Tourism: International Perspectives", in S.J. Page and D. Getz (eds.), The Business of Rural Tourism: International Perspectives, pp. 3-37, London: International Thomson Business Press.

Ramarao, R. (2012), "Competitiveness of India's Micro and Small Enterprises through Functional Competencies: Role in Nation's Development", *Vikalpa,* 37(1), 97-111.

Rola-Rubzen, M.F., Gibbs, J., Gabunada, F., Burritt, R., Altangerel, D., Fung, L., Rubzen, B. and Carter, A. (2011), "Growing Businesses in the Desert: Case Studies of Australian Desert Micro, Small and Medium Enterprises", Alice Springs: Ninti

One Ltd.

Schumpeter, J.A. (1934), "The Theory of Economic Development: An Inquiry into Profits, Capital, Credit, Interest and the Business Cycle", Cambridge, MA: Harvard University Press.

Shaw, G. (2004), "Entrepreneurial Cultures and Small Business Enterprises in Tourism", in A. Lew, M. Hall and A.M. Williams (eds.), A Companion to Tourism, pp. 291-302, Oxford: Blackwell.

Shen, F., Hughey, K.F.D. and Simmons, D.G. (2008), "Connecting the Sustainable Livelihood Approach and Tourism: A Review of the Literature", *Journal of Hospitality and Tourism Management,* 15, 19-31.

Sterren, J. (2008), "Financial Markets, Microfinance and Tourism in Developing Countries", available at: http://www.arajournal.net/files/pdf/article/ca_ES/32.pdf.

Thomas, R. (2004), "International Perspectives on Small Firms in Tourism: A Synthesis", in R. Thomas (ed.), Small Firms in Tourism, pp. 1-12, Oxford: Elsevier.

Tinsley, R. and Lynch, P. (2001), "Small Tourism Business Networks and Destination Development", *International Journal of Hospitality Management,* 20(4), 367-378.

Tourism and Transport Consult International (2011), "New Directions for Tourism in the West", available at: http://www.itic.ie/fileadmin/docs/New_Directions_-__Final.pdf.

UNESCAP (2005), "Major Issues in Tourism Development in the Asian and Pacific Region: Enhancing the Role of Tourism in Socio-economic Development and Poverty Reduction", Bangkok: UNESCAP.

Vellas, F. (2011), "The Indirect Impact of Tourism: An Economic Analysis", available at: http://dtxtq4w60xqpw.cloudfront.net/sites/all/files/111020-rapport_vellas_en.pdf.

World Tourism Organisation (1995), "Collection of Tourism Expenditure Statistics", Madrid: WTO.

World Travel and Tourism Council (2006), "Greece: The Impact of Travel and Tourism on Jobs and the Economy", London: WTTC.

Zortuk, M. (2009), "Economic Impact of Tourism on Turkey's Economy: Evidence from Co-integration Tests" *International Research Journal of Finance and Economics,* 4(25), 231-239.

Index

Index

W

Y